Nurturing the Sanctified Imagination of Urban Youth

Annie Lockhart-Gilroy

Urban Loft Publishers | Skyforest, CA

Nurturing the Sanctified Imagination of Urban Youth

Urban Loft Publishers
P.O. Box 6
Skyforest, CA 92385
www.urbanloftpublishers.com

Senior Editors: Stephen Burris & Kendi Howells Douglas
Copy Editors: Christian Arnold & Brittnay Parsons
Graphics: Brittnay Parsons
Cover Design: Elizabeth Arnold

ISBN-13: 978-1-949-625-23-3

Made in the U.S

This book is dedicated to the memory of my brothers:
Ivan Eric Edmunds
and
Eddie Leonard Lockhart

Table of Contents

Acknowledgements

First, I give honor and praise to God who called me to this journey. I have not always been particularly happy about this call, but I am grateful and humbled to know that the Creator has a task for me to do. Part of my call is this book. There are many that have supported me, prayed for me, and kept me sane throughout this process. I am humbled by the number of people that have taken time to help me along this process, and am unable to name them all, but there are some that have gone above and beyond whom I must mention by name.

I am forever grateful to my immediate family: My mother, Melanie Lockhart; my brothers Ivan Edmunds and Eddie Lockhart; and my nieces and nephews Jahkeem Lockhart, Asani Edmunds, Aza Edmunds, Jaden Lockhart, and Nori Lockhart. Not only have I been blessed with a great biological family, but also a wonderful group of sisters who choose to be my family. To Bridgett Green who provided regular pep talks throughout this process and to Kimberly Strange-Shanks, Erin Hayes, and Yvette McKoy, who constantly held me in prayer: Thank you. I also have the privilege of being able to call James Withers my brother from another mother. Thank you for your constant words of support and encouragement—as unconventional as they might be.

This work grew out of my dissertation, so I thank my dissertation committee, especially my advisor, Dr. Reginald Blount who guided and pastored me through the PhD process and beyond, while always making sure that the voice in this piece was completely and whole-heartedly mine. I often wanted to say, "Just tell me what to say and do!" But he wouldn't. Thank you for helping me claim my authentic voice. To Dr. Jack Seymour who was never discouraging after reading some questionable drafts as I was trying to find my way and then reading every chapter again as I continued to revise, rework, and rethink. Thank you. And to Dr. Evelyn Parker. When I first read Parker's book, I knew that that was the kind of work I wanted to produce. I am still a little starstruck whenever I see her, and I am grateful for her mentorship.

I have been blessed with great scholarly mentors. Dr. Kenda Creasy Dean took me under her wing while I was completing my master's degree. Though I had never seen myself as a scholar, she saw something in me I did not yet see, and for that, I am grateful. Dr. Richard Osmer was the first scholar to tell me that I should do PhD work. I thank both you and Kenda for the full court press. Once I arrived at the PhD program, I was taken in by Black women scholars. Thank you to Dr. Gennifer Brooks and Dr. Pamela Lightsey. I am also grateful for the many faculty members who regularly engaged me in conversation as I thought through this work: Dr. Margaret Ann Crain, Dr. Virginia Lee, Dr. Stephen Ray, and Dr. Nancy Bedford. Thank you. It is truly an honor to be encouraged by the people whose work I admire.

I am also grateful for the community that I found myself in while working at Drew University Theological School. Dr. Lynne Westfield provided much encouragement as well as constant motivation. I am also grateful to Dr. Traci West who pushed me along in the process by asking me to set deadlines and reading my work as I went along. And I am grateful for the pastoral mentorship of Bishop Peter Weaver and my thinking partner, Kimberliegh Jordan. The work of my research assistants was indispensable. Thank you, Gerard Jameson and Kyle Miller-Shawnee. I am also grateful to Javier Viera and the Louisville Institute for giving me the space of a post-doctoral fellowship to fine tune this work.

I am also grateful to the various church families that have seen me through this process: Ujima Village Christian Church, First United Methodist Church, Kingston United Methodist Church, and Faith United Methodist Church. To the youth group of Ujima Village Christian Church, thank you for sharing your lives with me and teaching me how to minister. To Pastor John Norwood and Deacon Tanya Norwood: I don't know if there are words to express the level of support you have given me. Thank you for going above and beyond in your support of my ministry to youth and ministry of academia.

Finally, I am beyond thankful to my husband, Bernard HP Lockhart-Gilroy. He has been my constant support, providing encouragement, accountability, and much laughter. He has edited every page in this book at least three times, and knows more about youth ministry, Christian Education, and womanist theology, than any physicist ever needs to know. Your editing has made me a better writer, our conversations have made me a better scholar, and our partnership has made me a better person. Thank you.

Introduction

Urban Life and Urban Ministry

In the beginning of my career, I lived in two distinct professional worlds. From Monday to Friday I taught high school English at an independent school in an affluent suburb where parents paid over $25,000 a year (in 1998) for a high school education for their children. On the weekends, I worked nine miles away, where I directed a faith-based program for so-called "at-risk" teens that lived in a small city and its surrounding areas. These students were from poor and working-class families.

Over the years I realized that there were not as many differences between the two populations as my preconceived notions had led me to believe. Narratives fueled by stereotypes had led me to believe that there are more differences than similarities, but I found the reverse to be true. The independent school youth were better trained academically, but both groups possessed bright and gifted students. Both groups also possessed students with learning differences (although the city kids were rarely diagnosed). Both groups possessed students that loved to learn and students that preferred to be doing something else. I found myself doing similar projects to spark their interests.

While the young people[1] were similar in many ways, the differences showed up most starkly whenever we entered into any conversations about their future. The independent school kids had plans for bright futures that started, almost automatically, with higher education. Although the at-risk kids wished for bright futures as well, they had difficulty believing that those futures would actually come to fruition. The independent school kids had plans and looked upon a hopeful future with expectation. The at-risk kids had dreams and fantasies and looked upon their future with wistfulness. The at-risk kids knew there were options out there, but they did not believe that many of those options would be for them.

I often wondered why there was such a stark difference in how they saw their futures. The obvious – and too-easy – answer is socio-economic class. The idea that economically privileged adolescents have an advantage is not shocking, but too often we miss all the things that economic privilege buys. For not only does it buy things, it buys the belief that one *should* have those things. Class privilege does not only buy a fine education; it buys the belief that one *deserves* a fine education—almost as a birthright. Certainly, the groups had different experiences because of what money could buy. The independent school youth were well-travelled; they learned and played all over the world. The at-risk youth rarely travelled and regularly stayed within a 10-mile radius (with 10 miles being generous).

Students in both groups were involved in extra-curricular activities, but the focus of those activities were very different. My independent school kids were encouraged to do activities that would teach them a particular skill or train them for the future in some way. My at-risk kids were encouraged to do things that would keep them busy and out of trouble. My independent

---

[1] Throughout this book I use the following words interchangeably: teenagers, youth, young people, and adolescents. These terms have fluid connotations. "Adolescent" tends to be used in developmental psychology and used to describe anyone who has reached puberty but is not financially independent. With puberty starting earlier and earlier and financial independence starting later and later, the range of adolescence is expanding. "Youth" and "young people" tend to be used within youth ministry circles. Sociologists have also used "youth" to refer to college-aged individuals and "teenagers" for those ages 13-18. Since I write across all these disciplines, I use all these different terms. Within this project I am referring to individuals between the ages of 13 and 18.

school kids heard about career tracks built on passions, interests, and earning potential. My at-risk kids heard about job skills that would get them a decent job.

While my suburban kids were taught to be ambitious, my city kids were taught to be realistic. And because they were trained this way, many of my independent school kids looked to the future with nervous anticipation while many of my at-risk kids, if they looked forward at all, looked to the future with dread or apathy. Yet, they both looked towards a future that was fixed. If the independent school kids had a bright future as their birthright, what, then, was the birthright of the at-risk youth?

While each state defines the term "at-risk" differently, the term here falls in line with the definition put forth by The National Center for Education Statistics (NCES). The NCES lists the following factors that lead to an "at-risk" label for students:

1. low socioeconomic status;
2. living in a single-parent home;
3. changing schools at non-traditional times;
4. below-average grades in middle school;
5. being held back in school through grade retention;
6. having older siblings who left high school before completion; and
7. negative peer pressure.

It is important to note that of these seven criteria, only two of them are within any control of the youth, and those two—having below-average grades and repeating a grade—are so often symptoms of deeper problems that are also not in their control. These youth are considered at-risk not because of their choices or actions, but because of racist, sexist, and classist views in the wider culture. These kids are labeled at-risk because they were born into poor and working-class families, with the majority of them being Black and Latinx families led by women. Does this label, then, become their birthright?

The notion of birthright should take on a different tone when seen through the lens of Christian theology. Yet, I could not always clearly distinguish the believers from the non-believers when speaking about their futures. Furthermore, there was little difference in the essence of the conversation about one's lot in life between the youth in the faith-based program and some of the youth in my church youth group. They used the same room at the same church and were from similar backgrounds. For the most part, they were "good" kids that didn't get into a lot of trouble, but their background made many of them fall into the "at-risk" category. And they too, embodied this label. They spoke a different language when speaking about their future. While my program kids would say, "It's not where you come from, it's where you are going," my youth group kids would say, "God has a plan for me, so God will make a way—somehow." They wanted to believe it, but many did not believe it fully. I so badly wanted them to believe it.

So, I worked towards filling that gap. Like many urban ministers, I arranged college visits and took kids to college fairs. I held career panels, set up apprenticeships, and taught career planning. I created summer sessions that focused on college planning. I thought that if I could only expose them to the big world that is out there, they would want to be a part of it. After over a decade of doing this, I realized that something was deeply missing. I now had program alums and young adults in my congregations that still did not believe that they really had a right to partake in the opportunities that I was trying so desperately to expose them to.

It took me a while to realize that while I had good intentions, I had the wrong foundation, for it was not an articulated theological one. Without an articulated theological foundation, I had some nice events, but that was all. Without an articulated theological foundation, these events were all about a path to secular success. For me, the endgame was not that they go to college and get lucrative careers, but that they know that they could. I wanted them to believe that they had the same divine birthright as my independent school kids. I told them that God had big dreams for them, but my fear of sounding like a "prosperity-gospel preacher" left me inarticulate.

I didn't want to tell them that they were children of God, so they had the right to be secularly successful. I didn't want to focus on financial blessings or earthly success. This was not about career, but vocation. I wanted them to embark on a lifelong vocation, one that could occur once the limits that had been placed on them—and internalized by them—were addressed. I wanted them to imagine various possibilities and work towards those possibilities. I wanted them to have hope for their future.

What I needed was a practical theology that helped me answer this question: How do we prepare urban youth for their futures—not a future that is created for them, but one that is designed in partnership with God? This book seeks to answer that question by describing a youth ministry rooted in nurturing the sanctified imagination of urban youth.

This book, therefore, is for those who work with youth that for one reason or another feel hopeless. My hope is that this text gives you a way of fostering hope by nurturing their imagination so that they can live into a personal future that is divinely inspired. I believe that youth can transform their lives and therefore transform their neighborhoods and their cities, and when a congregation imagines together, they can work together to transform their current reality.

Pitfalls to Avoid

While I make this argument, I strive to stay away from three pitfalls. First, I want to stay away from the pitfall of suggesting that all urban communities need is a change of practice and attitude. This text focusses on what congregations can do when youth and adults work together, think theologically, and imagine *together*. This does not mean that transformation of city kids' realities can only happen by these young people and the adults that work directly with them. Many of the problems of the most vulnerable in cities are a result of systematic oppression. Historically, city infrastructures were designed with no consideration for the poorest areas.

Simply look today at gentrification and relocation of a city's poorest people. Although I do not address these issues, I am mindful of them.

Second, thinking about how youth can transform their own communities does not absolve adults, organizations, or governments from responsibility or accountability. This is not a call to "pull oneself up by their own bootstraps." Nor is this a dismissal of the role that others play in the oppression of these urban centers. This book is a rallying cry! The rallying cry is for us to support youth that want to change their world and to encourage them. With partnership, we know they can make a difference. This is acclamation for congregations that are already imagining ways to live into the reign of God here on Earth. This is encouragement for those doing the work and food for thought for those who want to do the work but are unsure about where to start.

Third, I want to stay away from the pitfall of painting all urban youth with the same brush. The term "urban" is often used as a coded word for "Black," whether the Black person lives in Detroit, rural North Carolina, or upper-class Baldwin Hills. For many who fled the cities a generation or two ago, "urban" is equivalent to inner city, another coded word, that denotes a crime-ridden place where poor Black and Latinx people live. Usually, when people use the term urban, they are not imagining people that live in multimillion-dollar apartments on the Upper East side of Manhattan in New York City or on Lake Shore Drive in Chicago. Cities, however, are diverse places, with people from many walks of life. When I say "urban," I recognize the diversity within Black life and within actual cities, and I realize that no one book can speak to all of the constituents in a city or all the parishioners that may be a member of an urban congregation.

Therefore, when I speak of urban, I speak with particular persons in mind—the youth with whom I have worked. I do not think of statistics and generalities. I think of faces and particular stories. For almost twenty years, I have had the privilege and burden of walking with young people through some very difficult situations. As a counselor, teacher, coach, and youth minister, I have walked beside youth from dysfunctional families, unsafe homes, violence-plagued and drug-infested neighborhoods, and inadequate school systems, just to name a few situations. I have also danced at going-away-to-college parties, cheered at graduations and award ceremonies, and beamed with pride at musicals, concerts, and sporting events. I recognize that there is pain and joy in the city—as there is anywhere else. Yet, my ministry was often overwhelmed with pain as I walked beside teens desperately trying to imagine a different future for themselves. I have seen bright, determined, and talented young people lose hope and come to see imagining a different life as a futile endeavor. They instead, at a very early age, settle for making the best of what they have instead of imagining something different.

These are the experiences I bring forth in my stories. These are the people I think of when, in this context, I use the term urban. And most of these people are Black. Therefore, while urban is not code for Black, these are the youth I have worked with and most of my references speak to Black experiences and the experience of other marginalized folk. As I work with these texts, I will speak from a particular understanding of Black urban life.

A Fusion of Methods: Listening to both Theology and Experience

As I go forth in this work, womanist theory and theology serve as my way of knowing (epistemology) and personal, systematic reflection. Autoethnography serves as my primary methodology. Womanist scholars approach their work using a variety of methods. Because womanist theology centers on the lives and experiences of black women and use that as a basis for theological reflection, a common methodological starting point is to start with a Black woman's story.[i] Stephanie Mitchem argues that this is a necessary starting point because "womanist theology begins with life experiences and ordinary theologies to name the location of holiness in black women's lives."[ii] For this reason many womanist works include autobiographical portions. Following in that vein, this text is autoethnographic in nature.

Autoethnography is so named because it seeks to understand a cultural experience through the analysis and interpretation of personal experience. Therefore, following Heewon Chang, my use of autoethnography is, "ethnographic in its methodological orientation, cultural in its interpretive orientation, and autobiographical in its content orientation."[iii] My story does not exist in and of itself. Constant in the practice of autoethnography is the understanding that "individual stories are framed in the context of the bigger story, a story of the society."[iv] My story is one of a youth minister and scholar seeking ways to nurture imagination in a population that is so desperately trying to hold on to it.

As I bring forth my stories and experience as well as recognize the diversity of urban ministry experiences, I take "intersectionality" seriously. Coined by critical race theorist Kimberlé Crenshaw, intersectionality is a method of studying the relationships among multiple identities such as race, class, and gender. Viewing urban youth through the understanding of intersectionality further allows us to see the different nuances of the people that fall under this term. This concept helps us to examine the complexities that exist in one person's identity and how discriminatory practices against different populations are related. Those that live in urban environments come from a variety of places and have a variety of backgrounds. The stories I tell in this book come from my experience with youth from different ethnic and economic backgrounds and different genders. The intersections that they embody are kept in the foreground of my mind because it helps for a richer, more in depth, and more meaningful analysis. Keeping intersectionality at the foreground of urban ministry also helps the term "urban" to not be seen as coded language for Black and Latinx, poor, problematic, uneducated, or any other monolithic stereotype.

Too often, whenever I tell someone that I have spent much of my career in urban ministry, I either get looks of sympathy or admiration for my "bravery." There is an immediate image of my swerving past "drive-bys" every day on my way to work. I will not deny the difficulties and dangerous aspects of ministry in particular parts of the city, but my experience is a much broader picture.

My experience in urban ministry has been working primarily with Black youth. Within and among Black communities, there is great diversity and issues of differences based on class, gender, education, ability, theology, and the many identity aspects that make us who we are. Understanding intersectionality encourages ministering to the whole person. So, while one may have to speak in broad strokes, one cannot minister that way. Not only is the concept of intersectionality needed to embrace and discuss one's full identity, but it is also needed as we continue to push for social justice. Through the lens of intersectionality, social problems can be analyzed more fully, more effective intervention can be created, and inclusive advocacy can be promoted.

Looking Ahead

So, I move forward with the faces of my youth in front of me as I write about our shared stories.

- In Chapter One I discuss two problems I have encountered in my work in urban youth ministry—the communal problem of crippling nostalgia which contributes to the individualistic problem of personal hopelessness. This is my contextual frame. Therefore, I will discuss the plight of youth in this context. As I tease out these concerns, I introduce and suggest the solution of embracing of the sanctified imagination.
- The description of this imagination is then defined and expounded upon in Chapter Two.
- Chapter Three turns to one of the communities that ought to nurture this sanctified imagination—the Christian congregation. I discuss the emancipatory ecclesiology needed to nurture the sanctified imagination.
- In Chapter Four I explore the importance of local congregations being intentionally intergenerational and explore what it would

mean to have bi-directional mentoring in an intergenerational setting.

- Chapter Five envisions Christian Education through the lens of sharing wisdom as I review Christian Education practices that help nurture the imagination. I review different methods of critical pedagogy in order to show the various ways imagination can be nurtured through the teaching ministry of the Church.
- I end with a sending forth. I imagine what it would look like to incorporate all the aforementioned aspects and help nurture a young person's sanctified imagination.

I must admit that I have struggled with the scope of this work. At times, it feels too broad. "The book can't cover *everything*" is what I kept saying to myself, "There are too many topics." However, the more I sought to narrow, the more those pieces begged me not to remain on the editing room floor. Certainly, this book does not cover *everything*, but I did choose breadth, opting to paint a panorama instead of a smaller scene.

There are a lot of pieces needed for nurturing the sanctified imagination. The pieces presented here can be seen as portions of a quilt that make perfect sense on their own, but when placed together with the other complementary pieces, form a unique and powerful project. It would be possible for each of these chapters to function as standalone articles in their own right. One could look at a particular chapter and focus on that alone for their congregation for a while or place it in conversation within a wider discussion, but when placed together, it forms a rich tapestry that needs every piece it has to be the complex project that it is. So, I present the beginning of many conversations that I hope will continue throughout my career. I invite your responses too. As we work together with youth, we can build a context of hope and possibility. We can be fueled by the sanctified imagination. We can see where theological reflection and personal experience embody vocation.

Chapter 1

The Problems of Crippling Nostalgia and Personal Hopelessness

For many years, I ministered in a city that had once been great. I say that not to be pejorative but historically descriptive. It had been a leading city in manufacturing in the early 1900s. Its many factories had made it a strong economic city. But by the 1970s, the manufacturing economy had declined, leaving behind empty factories that remain abandoned to this day. There has been no shortage of attempts to revitalize the city and bring it back to its glory days. As I listened to conversation after conversation about how to revitalize the city, I was always struck by the language used. The language always involved going backwards and reclaiming an identity of the past. The nostalgia for the good old days made people want to bring back things that made them strong. A voice would then bring new ideas to the table, maybe something that has worked in another city, or an idea that just came to them. These ideas would be entertained only briefly as the conversation reverted to how things used to be and if only we could get the same kind of economy and communal structure again.

In many ways, I could call this city "Small City, USA" for these stories are replicated across the country. Many small cities have found themselves relying on one or two major employers that provide middle class income for blue collar workers. When that employer or employers shut down, the first question is: "Who can we get to come in and use these factories/mines/mills/refineries/etc. and take us back to the booming economy we used to know?" This question can linger for years and decades.

Indeed, small cities are not the only places that struggle this way. This type of thinking is nationwide. Yet, residents and leaders of small cities find themselves in an in-between place. They are not the charming Norman Rockwell-esque small towns that are often depicted as salt of the earth, hardworking, "real Americans" that make our country strong. They are also not the big cities that are seen as brimming with opportunity and inspire songs and movies about making it in such a place. Small cities carry the weight of being seen as crime-ridden places without the benefits of the glitz and glamour of a large city.

So, when someone in a meeting talked about a successful project in another city, someone would quickly remind the group about all the things that the other city had that their particular small city did not. And once again talk would cycle back to nostalgic conversation about the past; this cycle seems like a never-ending loop that lasts in meeting after meeting after meeting. This is *crippling nostalgia* that squelches the hope to explore new possibilities.

The term "nostalgia" was coined by Johanness Hofer[v] in the late 17th century and was meant to describe a condition of extreme homesickness among Swiss soldiers fighting far away from home. The term is from the Greek words *nostos* (to return home) and *algia (*pain or longing). "Nostalgia is a longing for a home that no longer exists or has never existed."[vi] It became to be viewed as a disease and the common cure was to either return home or be given the promise of returning home — regardless of whether that promise was real. By the 20th century the term had evolved to mean a longing not so much for a place, but for a time. And instead of being seen as painful, it was seen as comforting and actually remembering without pain. In fact, nostalgia became defined as an idealized memory where the hurtful parts of the memory were taken away and it became a longing for a past that was not being remembered truthfully.[vii] The accuracy of the memory became irrelevant. The ability to actually go back to the time or to recreate what is remembered as the greatness of the time also became irrelevant. The only relevant piece of nostalgia is the positive sentimental feelings that are evoked when one remembers. In the common lexicon, few would see nostalgia as a disease but more as wistful longing. However, I contend that constant communal nostalgia is damaging enough to be seen as a community disease. Referring to this longing for the past as *crippling nostalgia* takes the term to its original meaning.

Nostalgia is commonly seen as a fond memory for a time gone by. Many confuse nostalgia with history or memory. However, nostalgia is not a complete memory. Sean Gammon said it well when he noted, "Of course not all nostalgia is concocted or manipulated to gild our pasts—though much is, leaving us, analogously, with little more than edited highlights of a game that probably never took place."[viii] Part of the desire to escape to the past is the comfort that nostalgia gives. It feels like known territory, often because it is recreated in one's brain as what one wanted it to be more so than what it actually was. But nostalgia is crippling for exactly this reason. We often see the past through rose-colored glasses. For example, some small cities *were* more economically prosperous, but people worked under terrible conditions. Laws that limit child labor, require basic decency in the workplace, and mandate a livable wage are all good things. Lamenting a mostly mythical nostalgic time gone by tempts us to ignore social progress. Things are much better for children, women, and ethnic minorities, and that is a good thing. Though some link social progress to the downfall of a city, that is an ahistorical analysis.

While many people point to past economic stability, it is also important to remember that the economic structure of a small city often was not prosperous for everyone. "Thus nostalgia, as a historical emotion, is a longing for that shrinking 'space of experience' that no longer fits the new horizon of expectations."[ix] A crippling nostalgia excuses the horror of the past because it allows us to escape from our current problems.

This nostalgia also cripples because constantly wanting the same things of the past limits our ability to imagine new possibilities and move forward.

"The nostalgic desires to obliterate history and turn it into private or collective mythology, to revisit time like space, refusing to surrender to the irreversibility of time that plagues the human condition."[x] We cannot, in the same moment, both long for the past *and* imagine a new future. The stark reality is that those manufacturing jobs are not coming back. Even those that create plans to restore the jobs of the 1970s incorporate difficult working conditions and low wages that cannot provide a livable income.

These are not things we should yearn for. Instead, we should yearn for new ideas that would make lives better both economically and socially. This requires responding to crippling nostalgia with our God-given imaginations. Those living in areas where a crippling nostalgia is prevalent can respond in several ways: Some choose to reject the premise and become activists by responding with imaginative actions and programs. Others accept the premise and work towards bringing things back to the way they used to be. Yet, there are others that take crippling nostalgia to its logical conclusion: if the better days are behind us and we cannot get those back, only worse days lie in front of us. So, why should we work to bring forth anything? My work concentrates on youth within the third population.

Youth constructing their identity in an area where crippling nostalgia is prevalent have an even more difficult time navigating the way forward, for crippling nostalgia also cripples adolescent development. A constant refrain of "things were so much better in the past" affects the way youth in the community see their future. We call youth the future, but crippling nostalgia strips youth of the power to create that future. This communal construct explains, in part, why many of the youth I ministered to feared the future. This nostalgia also cripples youthful imagination. It assumes that there is a clear-cut answer to the problems around these young people and that this answer lives in the past – a past that youth have experienced, know nothing about, and therefore cannot contribute solutions, because they cannot help recreate this past for which they were not present. In the context of this communal crippling nostalgia, youth are trying to construct their personal identity. This can cause them to be unexcited when looking towards their future.

Identity Construction in a Community of Crippling Nostalgia and Miseducation

On my first day working with a group of young men in middle adolescence in a faith-based non-profit program, I saw a small group of Black young men who were both skeptical and anticipating the opportunities that this program could provide. After some quick introductory words, I could tell that they would be willing participants, as we spoke about goal setting. I started by wanting to separate attainable goals from fantasy or wishful thinking. So, after instructing them that we were going to do a goal setting exercise, I asked, "What would your life be like in your fantasy world? You have Oprah money and any situation that is holding you back can be removed. So, give me your wildest dreams of how you would like to be living 10 years from now." I sought to get the ball rolling by saying that I would own a private island, and of course a yacht to get to and from the island. And I would have to live somewhere, so I described the mansion that I would live in on this island.

It was a general "If you won the lottery, what would you do with the money?" conversation. One student talked about a private jet instead of a boat, but generally mimicked my answer. The others listed things that I thought were well within reach: a nice house, a steady job, owning one's own business, a great wardrobe with some designer clothes in it, etc. I noticed that their list entailed more goals than my outlandish list, so I said, "You guys are naming goals and moving ahead of me, but that's cool. Let's move from fantasy to realistic goals like the ones you were listing."

Then the list became more modest: a good job, a nice apartment, living in a safe neighborhood, etc. Still not understanding what was happening, I explained that those were all great and sensible goals, for the next few years, but I wanted to start with a finish line of ten years down the line. Something that you really had to reach for, but with hard work and planning would be well within your reach.

Then I learned that the first list *was* their fantasy list and the second list *was* their future goals list, and very few of them thought that they could achieve their list of goals. Most of them would be happy with being alive and out of trouble in 10 years. Owning a business and having a house in a safe neighborhood was, to them, pure fantasy. At that time, I thought that because these were youth labelled "at-risk", that they had particular circumstances that led them to this place, and I thought that was the reason for their bleak outlook on life. The more I worked with youth from this urban environment, the more that I saw that this bleak look was not limited to only a few. The conversations seemed so hopeless about the future.

Despite a rather bleak view of the future, youth with whom I worked were still able to find oases in society that gave them hope. The *idea* of hope is not a foreign concept for these youth: They spoke of hope in God and all the things that God could do. They spoke of how God could make a way out of no way, but they spoke of this in an abstract or corporate sense. God could make a way for some people, just not for them. God could do things in the abstract, but not on a personal level.

What they demonstrated was personal hopelessness. God could help other people; just not me. God could make a way out of no way in grand sweeping gestures, but getting me into college was either beneath God, not a concern, or not possible. This sense of personal hopelessness was worn like a protective suit of armor. It did not help you fight, but it helped you from getting damaged and getting hurt. Where did these youth learn, at such an early age, to avoid hope in order to not see their hopes dashed? How could one believe in a miracle-making God, but not believe that God would make miracles for them? This personal hopelessness is learned. It is formed within communal crippling nostalgia and cemented by other structures that teach these youth to fear their future.

The young children in the same community did not exhibit the same sense of hopelessness. Children are often inquisitive and full of wonder.

They constantly question how things work and why they work the way they do. Yet, this is not often encouraged as children get older. Many see the purpose of education — both formal and informal — as getting people to conform. Part of the education of conformity is the acceptance of current circumstance. Students are asked to conform to larger societal norms and their place within those norms. This often results in very limited knowledge. Nevertheless, passion for thinking opens up a world of possibilities for a child; educating solely for obedience and conformity closes that world and forces youth to believe that the world only holds a small place for them.

One's place in US culture is influenced by one's race, class, and gender. Young people learn this and "their place" from a variety of sources; one of those sources is their local public school. While in school, children learn many things beyond academic subjects—they learn how to construct their reality. They not only learn what they ought to know, but who they ought to be. And for so many of the youth that I worked with, the lesson learned was that they are limited. Youth construct their reality based on the world that they see. Therefore, before seeking to minister to youth in a way that helps them break out of a narrow way of thinking, one must first understand the reality they are constructing. This will differ in different contexts, yet several ethnographic studies have been conducted with urban youth that show particular trends.[2]

One such trend is youth constructing their neighborhood environments primarily as places to be escaped. The teens that hung on to hope, hoped for a way out. Sports and music were the primary ways youth saw as their way out. Sports and music could each lead to a lucrative career. Even more importantly, sports and music can help one afford college, for education is truly seen as the way out. Yet, education is often the source for keeping youth limited. When interviewing the students about the

---

[2] While there are many ethnographic research projects on this population, my work is informed by my own auto-ethnography and two texts: Loretta Brunious, *How Black Disadvantages Adolescent Socially Construct Reality: Listen, Do you Hear What I Hear?* (New York: The Continuum Publishing Company, 1996) and Julie Bettie, *Women Without Class: Girls, Race, and Identity* (Berkley: University of California Press, 2003).

importance of school, Loretta Brunious notes that many of the youth perceive schooling as a means to social and economic advancement in a very vague sense. In addition, they do not connect schooling with social empowerment, civic responsibilities, or as a means to a brighter future. Students were able to express the cultural understanding as to what school is "supposed" to be for (as in a passageway to college and future employment) but did not necessarily believe it to be true for them. "While the students can articulate the 'correct' cultural ideology about the value of education, they appear to be oblivious to their oppressed state."[x] When asked to imagine their dream school, the students describe a school that is clean and without graffiti, where teachers make learning fun.

Though such schools exist for many Americans, for these youth, it is a fantasy. Instead, they describe familiar school systems which run in a way that makes it hard to learn, as they themselves recognize. They share stories of teachers pre-judging them and being clear that little is expected of them. These stories paint a picture of schools that do not open avenues for youth, but instead close off options. These youth often attend schools that perpetuate the banking system of education[3] instead of educating in a way that encourages imagination and critical thinking.[4] The banking system demands conformity and obedience, even to a system that harms you. Imagination and critical thinking are key to challenging this harmful system. Yet, people still depend on this broken educational system as a way out even as it functions as a way to remain confined.

Another qualitative study conducted by Julie Bettie further adds to this conversation with her discoveries as expressed in *Women Without Class: Girls, Race, and Identity.* Many of the girls Bettie spoke to had been tracked into vocational education. As she travelled with the seniors on a field

---

[3] The concept of education as a banking system is discussed by Paulo Friere in his seminal work, *Pedagogy of the Oppressed (1968).* The term is a metaphor for seeing students as containers where educators simply deposit knowledge. This knowledge is then withdrawn for tests and exams. This type of pedagogy lacks critical thinking and merely serves to recreate the status quo.

trip to a nearby vocational business school, she noted how the representative explained to the students that instead of attending college, a more realistic goal for them was to get more vocational training. This vocational training is another way that poor urban students are limited. Both the vocational tracks at the high school and these vocational schools play on the strained economics of these youth. They claim to offer them a cheaper alternative to college and instead offer them a certificate that will land them jobs that may not pay enough to support themselves.

These youth are directed towards jobs that perpetuate the class status quo – a status quo perpetuated by the vocational tracks themselves, as it is often poor and working-class students and students of color who are placed in the vocational tracks. These tracked students often do not have the classes needed to enroll into state schools and universities, so an academic higher education has been removed as an option for them before they are old enough to decide if that is the path they want. If a student then decides to try to attend college, they need to attend a junior college to get the information or preparation that they should have gotten in high school. This adds financial strain to a student already struggling economically. This type of tracking institutionalizes socio-economic class and perpetuates the existing class structure.

Students are also often told that training is an answer, but they are often placed into programs that do not train them for jobs that pay living wages. Students are constantly told that there are these jobs out there that would pay enough to sustain a comfortable middle-class lifestyle, only if they would get trained. So, those who do get trained end up working hard to become a part of the working poor. Disturbingly, vocational tracks and training often perpetuate traditional gender roles. Bettie noted that girls were often encouraged to explore clerical jobs and cosmetology. As Bettie questioned girls about the discrimination in tracking, she noted, "Girls vacillated between understanding their dilemma, the circumstances of their lives that were resulting in precarious futures, and denial about it."[xi] Much like Brunious' observation and my own, Bettie notes that while students could name their dilemma, they could not necessarily recognize their oppressed state.

These youth have been placed in a precarious situation by the decisions of others. Not only do teens not choose their neighborhood, school district, nor socio-economic class; they have little agency and legal right in choosing these things. Yet, instead of having adults walk alongside them and aid them in imagining a variety of options for their lives, they are steered further on to a path that will keep them within the working class or working poor. At no point do I intend to suggest that there is something wrong with being working class; I, do however, believe that there is something wrong with youth being taught that being working class is their only option.

I object to *any* kind of teaching that closes doors instead of opening them. The more students hear that there are only certain things they can achieve, the more they believe and internalize it, the more they get a sense of personal hopelessness, and the more their perception of the future is crippled. Students can fight against the encroaching idea of crippling nostalgia that leads to personal hopelessness if they are trained to think critically about their situations, but many of these young people are not in educational institutions that teach for critical thinking that would encourage youth to go against the grain. The goal and outcome of many of these institutions is to reproduce the grain.

Schools like those studied by Brunious and Bettie may lead some to deplore public education within the United States without acknowledging the achievement gap. The educational achievement gap refers to the staggering difference in public school education between wealthier communities and low-income areas. The testing data of every state show radical differences between low-income student achievement and middle-class and upper-class suburban student achievement.

The academic achievement gap also runs along racial lines. For example, 83% of Asian American students and 78% of White students graduate from high school in four years, compared to 57% of African American and Latino/Hispanic students.[xii] In addition, 37% of Black fourth-graders cannot perform basic math skills, compared to only 10% of White students.[xiii] The achievement gap illustrates the battle that Black and Latinx students face as they construct their current identity and think about their future. The gap widens when socio-economic class and geography (urban vs. suburban) are considered.

Nicole Baker Fulgham, an educator and advocate for closing the academic achievement gap, highlights the profound impact the achievement gap has on students on the low side of the gap:

> *Taking a longer view, we see that public school inequity means more than contrasting crumbling inner-city school buildings with shiny, expansive high school campuses in the suburbs. It goes far beyond whether or not a school offers AP calculus. It stretches further that the disturbing reality that some schools fundamentally believe all students can achieve, while others seem to assume that poor children are destined for failure. What's the bottom line? Public school inequity affects what millions of students are able to do with their lives. Educational inequity profoundly impacts students' futures and, ultimately, their destinies.[xiv]*

The inequity between public schools—and even within public schools due to tracking—helps to enforce the idea not only that poor students cannot achieve, but that they should not achieve. Indeed, there are stories of those raised in poor neighborhoods who overcame the odds to achieve great success. These stories are often used to show that everyone can overcome the odds if they work hard enough. This approach forgets that if everyone "overcame the odds," there would no longer be odds to overcome. Barriers to success exist because the majority of those afflicted by educational inequity often see a different path and fewer options than those who are not. Educational inequity affects the way one constructs reality and profoundly impacts one's ability to envision a future for themselves. When youth begin to see themselves as having limited skills and limited options, they also see their future as limited.

Some students in the qualitative studies expressed their desire to attend a different school, but, among other things, gangs and gang affiliation limit where they can travel safely. This limits school choice. Nearly 80 percent of public-school students attend the school closest to their home. Therefore, the problems that plague their schools often speak to problems within their neighborhoods.

Another aspect of poor Black youth's construction of social reality is the fact that they often come of age in such violence-plagued communities. Being cultivated in poverty and violence means being confronted with negative images on a regular basis. "These 'social facts' are key components to the construction of their *common sense* world and their definition of Self."[xv] Being nurtured in a violent world creates a distinctive sense of self, sense of reality, and sense of what is possible. Imagining a different future for one's self can feel far removed from learning how to survive enough to get through the next day.

When students were asked how to avoid gangs, four different possibilities were given: you can't; move out of the neighborhood; stay in the house; and get into positive activities like sports.[xvi] The first three responses note the reality of the situation and express a belief that being in the neighborhood without being involved with gangs is essentially impossible. Gang presence creates a sense of reality that is limiting, manipulating, and constraining. By controlling a neighborhood, gangs convince neighborhood inhabitants not only that there is no way to stop them, but that there is no way to not be a part of them. The last response, however, shows that some students recognize a hopeful alternative. These responses prove that alternative stories of reality do exist and can be cultivated. The question then becomes, from where does this hope extend and how can this hope be fostered when so many young people feel cut off from other youth and communities?

These factors, among many others, lead to youth feeling very isolated. Gang violence physically limits where youth feel safe enough to travel and serves as a method of isolation. "Isolation has a resounding effect on the social construction of reality for black disadvantaged adolescents."[xvii] I would take students to museums and sights in their own small city and was often told that this was the first time they had been there or in that part of town. Many of the students had not explored the full eight square miles of their city. Some stated that they didn't think there were cool things like this in their city. They had been convinced that their small city did not have much to offer. Others did not have the funds to explore the different cultural areas of their city and others noted that certain neighborhoods were off limits because of gangs, or as one student put it, "people here don't like people from my part of town." Economics combined with violence cripple youth from exploring the world around them. This isolation also stops youth from seeing the many different options around them. If one's world is limited to their block or their area of town, they develop a very narrow view of what the world is and how life can be lived.

Brunious contends that overall, "this study reveals that the children in these communities are recipients of negative labeling processes, and as such, they have low-self-worth and their lives are plagued by negativism and inferiority."[xviii] It is from this standpoint that they construct their reality and learn what is possible in their lives. However, in order for people to enact their own agency, they need to see themselves worthy of that power; bell hooks argues that a low self-esteem is one of the major factors that still stop Blacks from fulfilling their true potential. "Without a core foundation of healthy self-esteem, we cannot practice self-love."[xix] And without self-love we do not know what we are capable of; we can be convinced to remain small. "Among poor children in our nation, especially the black poor, the message is taught early, 'Your life has no value—you are doomed.'"[xx] When internalized, these thoughts become the basis of a personal hopelessness and limited view of one's future.

Urban Realities and a Theology of Hope and Empowerment

Although this hopelessness is prevalent, it cannot have the last word. People of God are people of hope. And for many of the Black youth, they come from traditions steeped in hope, for hope was and remains a tool for survival. So certainly, one's youth ministry can be a place, an oasis, where people combat feelings of personal hopelessness and fight against the communal crippling nostalgia. A place where people can partially respond to limiting education, isolation, and poor self-worth—a place that responds to these challenges with an emancipatory education, community, and a strong sense of self.

This begins with how we understand the relationship between the future and the past. Nostalgia is not always about the past; for these communities, it is about being retrospective in order to understand the problems of the present and create a different future. The desire is healthy even though the mode is not. One cannot create a future while being stuck in the past, but as the saying goes, "those that do not know history are doomed to repeat it." Therefore, the answer is not to ignore the past, but to be critical of it and learn from it. For urban youth and communities, the concept of "sankofa" can be helpful here. Sankofa is an Akan symbol and a term in the Twi language that is exemplified by the saying *se wo were fi na woman sofa a yank* which translates to "it is not taboo to go back and fetch it." The concept of sankofa is symbolized by a mythical bird with its head turned backwards and its feet planted forward while holding an egg. The egg symbolizes the promise of the future.

This term and symbol are powerful when thinking about the problem of crippling nostalgia. The bird is moving forward. It is not afraid of the future and although it looks back, it is not longing for the past. Instead it is reflecting on the past so that we are not starting from scratch. Looking to the past reminds us that we have been in difficult situations before and God has seen us through those. So, what can we learn from this? As the bird holds the egg, it holds the promise—the future. This can be seen as holding the youth, but it is important to remember that while youth are adults of the future, they are currently present in the here and now and are capable of joining in the work of imagining a way forward.

For our purposes, imagine that the bird is the congregation in the urban community fighting against the work of communal crippling nostalgia. The act of moving forward is the work of youth and the imagination needed to fight personal hopelessness. The act of looking back reflects the wisdom needed from the elders. The delicate egg that is held is the theological imagination needed for the future. We do not know what this future will hatch, but God knows, and we work with God to imagine a liberating way forward.

To bring all these things together, I suggest grounding them in the notion of nurturing the sanctified imagination in these youth. In its most simplistic form, the sanctified imagination is a journey one goes through with God with the belief that things can be different and unlimited by societal constructs. This theological imagination not only recognizes that God can fix *the* world, but God can also fix *my* world and *my* community and work with *me* as an agent of that change. I use the term nurturing because youth already possessed imagination. They do not need anyone to give it to them. However, without nurturing, ideas created by this imagination amount to nothing but fancy. Through nurturing the sanctified imagination, youth can find realistic ways to claim their future with God and believe that it can actually happen.

Moving Forward with the Fragile Youth Protected

There is a comic strip that I used to display that showed a youth minister in their office. The youth minister looks overwhelmed going through piles on their desk. The clipboard holds news articles that cite teen pregnancy rates, teen drug use, and other sociological studies that would help this minister understand the context of his youth. Then an older man who is clearly clergy walks in and says something like, "So, do you want to be a *real* pastor one day?" It is funny and frustrating because it is true. Many see youth ministry as a simple task of games, Sunday School, and different overnight trips, not real pastoring. But those that work in youth ministry know the heaviness of the work and all the information a youth minister juggles and carries to serve their youth well. Youth ministry can be a bit of a minefield, and urban youth ministry has its own special set of mines. I have laid out only a few of these mines. Yet, it is still overwhelming. But serving youth in this minefield is not impossible. It is possible to do it and do it well. The goal of this text is to disarm these mines with a theological response that is both insightful and motivational.

In the next chapter, I focus on the concept of the sanctified imagination. What is it? How is it helpful? What does it look like? This last question is the crux of the chapters that will follow. The task before us is large and daunting, but possible. So, let us journey together as we prepare to help young people and each other navigate this minefield and disarm landmines.

Chapter 2

The Sanctified Imagination

As a high school teacher, my favorite assignment to give was a project I called "The Protest Paper/Project." It started one year after reading *All Quiet on the Western Front, To Kill A Mockingbird,* and *Black Boy.* We talked about how one writes about the horrors of the world whether they are war, racism, or one of the world's many other problems. We talked about different approaches writers take to address the horrors of their day. Some tell moving and poignant stories that gently nudge the reader in a particular direction, while others take a more direct approach.

Some students wanted to know if they could do that too – write about problems in their worlds. First, I said, in order to do it well, one must know the complications and nuances of a particular issue. Riveted by the conversation, I re-envisioned the research project requirement and assigned the protest paper and presentation. They were to pick any problem in the world, tell us why it was problematic, and offer solutions and strategies for correction.

It was wonderful to see students catch on fire as they learned and informed each other about different societal concerns. By the time of the presentation, they were able to explain the issue they were addressing in detail, explain its problematic nature, and present it in creative and artistic ways. However, when it came to actions needed, their solutions were huge and beyond a person's involvement. Solutions required law changes, government interventions, and large-scale campaigns. Again and again, I was told that the only thing an individual could do was donate money to the cause. These students wanted to make a change; they just didn't know how. They saw the problem as being way too big for them as individuals and, in some ways, hopeless.

So, the assignment morphed. In its latest incarnation, I asked them to identify a community problem—something that affects them daily. This alone can take a little work. It is easy to think about climate change, for example, as a major issue; it is not always evident how it affects one personally. Through our discussions we teased out some of these issues. Then I asked them to research solutions on three levels.

1. What can be done as a nation or through global leadership?
2. What can be done as a school or neighborhood community?
3. What can be done as individuals?

They were also to research ways they could participate in the national and neighborhood changes. These changes to the assignment helped to keep the fires lit. Not only were students passionate about issues; they became passionate about what they could do.

My goal was to help nurture their imagination. While this project was in a secular school, there was a sense of making changes for a bigger purpose. When I had these conversations with youth in Christian environments, many of the same themes echoed throughout the conversations. Again and again, I spoke with teens who wanted to fix what was wrong in the world—even those that saw their own personal circumstance as hopeless.

One of the most common phrases that come from the mouths of young people is, "That's not fair!" And adults throughout out the ages have passed on the response, "Well, life is not fair!" This response is meant to portray reality, but it also portrays complacency. At some point in our development we have moved from desiring fairness to accepting, perpetuating, and sometimes championing unfair behavior while asking youth to simply deal with it. At some point between our own cries of "that's not fair" and our shrugs of complacency with a response of "Life is not fair," some forget a key thing—while life is often not fair, it *should* be.

Theological imagination seeks to harness the desire of youth for things to be fair and right and just. For that, in part, is what it means to participate in the reign of God.

It is not fair that children starve while there is enough food to feed everyone.

It is not fair that prisons are planned and built based on the standardized tests of fourth graders.

It is not fair that one is labeled "at risk" because of factors beyond their control.

It is not fair that teenagers have been convinced that they are forever stuck in situations that are not of their own making.

And like the latest evolution of the protest paper/project, this understanding of fair and right are large global and national problems that are also deeply personal. Too often, class and race privilege allow some of us to forget that there are actual human beings that suffer because of these large problems. Class privilege protected the independent school youth that I did this project with until I required them to make it personal. Several of the youth I ministered to did not have this class and race protection. They had less than enough to eat, traversed the school-to-prison pipeline's educational systems, been labeled "at risk," and felt stuck in their situation. These were not abstract issues; these were personal.

The truth of an unfair life should not be presented as something that must be accepted, but as something that ought to be challenged. Youth can be set on fire to transform their life and their world when there are adults that enable them to do so. Personal hopelessness can be combatted with communal imagination. Nurturing the sanctified imagination allows youth and their communities to have discussions about how to make the world fairer and discern the way to move forward and create a different path.

The Power of Imagination

The first time I heard the term "the sanctified imagination," I was in church listening to the sermon when the preacher stated, "Now allow me to use my sanctified imagination" as he began to talk about the unwritten possibilities within the Scripture passage. Having heard it several times since then, the term continues to strike me as profound. It presents the fact that the imagination could not only fill in the blanks of the written text in fun ways, but that the imagination could teach as it helps us see things in a different way, things that were not seen before. Imagination in and of itself is a powerful tool, but when it is sanctified, it takes on a whole new dimension. We are able to see God and the works of God in a new way.

The power of imagination runs all throughout the Hebrew and Christian Scriptures. From the very beginning—the creation story—we are presented with a God who imagines a different reality from the one existing and who works towards bringing that new reality into being. As the story continues and God begins to call people, God continuously calls them to live into a new reality. God calls Noah to make something that he has not seen before in preparation for an event he has yet to witness. God calls Abraham to journey with God and go to a place that is not yet revealed; God simply calls Abraham to travel to a place that will soon be revealed. God calls the people of Israel out of bondage into a new land before they are able to picture what it means to be free. God is constantly calling people to see things not yet seen, for we are called not to only see things through our eyes, but through God's eyes. Imagining a different reality with God often means journeying to a place that is not yet revealed.

As humans, we walk forth with God, aiding in bringing forth the reign of God. For God still calls us to create new realities and it is the Church's job to journey with God as we create these new realities. This requires us to see the future not as a fixed entity that will happen whether or not we act, but to see the future as a journey we take with God – something that we have the agency to enact. This is theological imagination. Before being able to see how the imagination works as sanctified, we must first see the imagination as theological.

To further define theological imagination, I build upon the work of Delores Williams and her use of the biblical story of Hagar and the wilderness experience.[5] The story of Hagar is told in Genesis 16 and 21. Sarai was barren and aged and did not believe that she would give birth to Abram's son. So, she gave Hagar, her slave, to Abram so Hagar could bear Abram's son. When Hagar became pregnant, Sarai despised Hagar and treated her harshly. Hagar ran away and returned, upon instruction of the angel of God. Hagar gives birth to Ishmael; later, Sarai and Abram (now Sarah and Abraham) conceive Isaac. When Sarah sees Ishmael playing, she becomes enraged, complains to Abraham, and asks Abraham to cast out Hagar and Ishmael so that Ishmael does not share in Isaac's inheritance. Hagar and her son are cast out by Abraham, and Hagar wanders in the wilderness. When her provisions are gone, she sits her son down, goes away from him (so that she does not hear her son cry nor see him die), and weeps. Again, an angel of the Lord comes to her. The angel tells her that God has heard the cries of her son. She is told to lift up her son and hold fast, for God will make a great nation out of him. God opened her eyes and she saw a well of water. From that well, she is able to nourish her child while in the wilderness.

Through the retelling and analysis of the story, Williams explores various notions of the wilderness experience and argues for naming the experience of Africans in America as the Survival/Quality-of-Life Tradition. When discussing the wilderness experience, Williams notes that there are two historical understandings within different historical periods in African American culture: the wilderness as sacred space and the wilderness as hostile, unfriendly, and threatening. Both expressions of the wilderness come together in the story of Hagar. The retelling of the Hagar story is helpful to our work with urban youth. Many of them are forced to construct

---

[5] A more in-depth study of how I use the Delores Williams's work can be found in my article written for the Religious Education journal: Annie Lockhart-Gilroy, "A Way Forward: Nurturing the Imagination at the Intersection of Race, Class, Gender, and Age," *Religious Education* 111, no. 4 (July 2016): 415-429.

a social reality that is a wilderness experience. They exist in a place of physical isolation where they live in fear because certain parts of their environments are often hostile, unfriendly, and threatening. Gangs manifest as a way of seeking to conquer this wilderness and obtain some sense of control. Like the pioneers exploring the western territories of the United States, the gangs attempt to conquer and control the wilderness which leads to destroying others in their wake. Youth are then forced to suffer the consequences in this wilderness. However, as Williams notes, the wilderness is not *only* hostile, unfriendly, and threatening. In the midst of this wilderness, God can also create sacred space and lessons for survival. For, in the end, Hagar finds her means of survival in the very wilderness in which she faced destruction. Williams credits Hagar's survival to a "new vision" that she receives from God. After her experience with God, she sees a well she had not seen before. This well is the God-given source of her survival. For youth living in the wilderness today, theological imagination can serve as their new vision—an additional God-given source of survival that will enhance their quality of life. As pockets of urban youth continue to find their way in the wilderness, it is within the responsibility of the body of Christ to help these young people to collectively see their new vision. I view this task of the Church as nurturing a theological imagination that is both liberating and transformative.

Conditioned to construct a problematic reality, many youth have been stripped of the power of their imagination. As bell hooks notes, "In dominator culture the killing off of the imagination serves as a way to repress and contain everyone within the limits of the status quo."[xxi] Having suffered the killing of one's ability to imagine a different life, one is left with the belief that one's perceived reality is not only an acceptable option, but the only true option. Therefore, to see a new vision, this imagination needs to be rekindled. "Imagination is one of the most powerful modes of resistance that oppressed and exploited folk can and do use."[xxii]

Imagination gives agency.

Imagination gives hope.

Imagination allows people to see their faith in new ways.

Imagination decolonizes the mind, replaces what has been stripped, and rekindles a natural inquisitive exploring tendency found in children but suppressed as children get older.

bell hooks further argues that we live in a world where children are asked to imagine, draw, create games, and have imaginary friends, but when they get older, "imagination is seen as dangerous, a force that could possibly impede knowledge acquisition."[xxiii] Indeed imagination *does* impede the passive acquisition of knowledge. Imagination encourages students to challenge, question, and ask how things can be different. Imagination is dangerous because it disrupts the status quo. Engaged with critical thinking, this imagination can lead one to then enact this differently imagined world.

The Power of the Sanctified Imagination

As we think about imagination, it is helpful to think about how God uses our imagination to cause us to see things differently. What does it mean for us to have a sanctified imagination? Sanctification is a Christian doctrine that is most simplistically defined as being made holy. Like all theological doctrines, one's understanding of this term depends on one's larger theological perspective. I explore this term from a Wesleyan perspective. John Wesley spoke of sanctification and holiness in many ways. For our purposes, I focus on three Wesleyan concepts and describe them briefly: sanctification as part of God's grace, sanctification as perfect love, and sanctification as social holiness.

First, when Wesley spoke of how one became Christian, he spoke of God drawing us through a three-fold understanding of grace: prevenient grace, justifying grace, and sanctifying grace. Being transformed into being who God intends for us to be is a lifelong process. It begins when we are born and before we are even aware of God. That is God's prevenient grace. As we begin to become aware of God and our need for God, we can experience God's justifying grace. And as we continue to live our lives, we can grow closer and closer to who God wants us to be— thus experiencing God's sanctifying grace. Viewing sanctification as the third leg of this process of God bringing us closer to holiness and who we were meant to be also views sanctification as a gift from God. Sanctifying grace is a gift freely given from God that allows us to be different—more like God. With this different way of being, we also have a different way of seeing. We desire to see things the way God sees things. With this gift of sanctifying grace, we are always growing and desiring more and more to be like God and to please God. Therefore, we can no longer be content with the way things are; we seek to please God in a new way. So, the sanctified imagination is used to see new ways—God-inspired new ways.

Wesley also spoke of sanctification as perfect love.[xxiv] As Wesley spoke of love, he spoke of love of God and love of neighbor. These two could not be separated. As one thinks about the gift of sanctifying grace the natural response is to respond with one's love of God. The fruit of this love of God is love of neighbors and love of every being God has created. We show that we love God by loving our neighbors.[xxv] If one loves God, one loves their neighbor, and if one loves their neighbor, one wants what is best for their neighbor and their neighborhood. Everyone who loves the God that created us will also love everyone that God created. Holiness, therefore, is not something to be developed privately, but in community. Wesley is often quoted for saying "There is no holiness but social holiness."[xxvi] While solitude and personal holiness is a part of the Christian faith, it cannot be the heart of the Christian faith, for Christianity is a faith that is lived out in the world and, therefore, must include social holiness. Another necessity of Christianity is peacemaking and doing good. Good Christian works are all works of mercy and part of the call of sanctification.[xxvii] These characteristics also do not exist in solitude; they must exist in society. As we live out our holiness in society, we also try to make society look more like God would have it look—free of the injustices that often lock urban youth into a particular status quo.

Viewing these three things as part of sanctification, the sanctified imagination is then an imagination gifted by God that enable us to be more like God and see the world through God-colored glasses so that we can participate in making the world look more like the world God created – a world where people are free to be the people God created them to be. People cannot be the people God created them to be if they are oppressed by another. They cannot be who God created them to be if they see limited realities.

There are many ways one can nurture their sanctified imagination. To hone this concept a little more I refer to the work of Kwok Pui-lan in her aim to define the theological imagination necessary for post-colonial people. While the context is not the same, there is much to be gleaned from this work. In her broadest definition, Kwok notes "to imagine means to discern that something is not fitting, to search for new images, and to arrive at new patterns of meaning and interpretation."[xxviii] My work with urban youth helped me to discern that something was definitely not fitting. The work of urban youth ministry, then, is to help youth defy old images, explore new ones, and arrive at new patterns. Kwok discusses three types of imagination that would aid us to arrive at these new patterns; for our purposes, we will focus on two: historical imagination and diasporic imagination.

In Kwok's discussion on historical imagination, she refers to Delores Williams's work with the historical figure of Hagar and notes that by exploring this figure she is lifting up a historical prototype to lift up aspects of Black women's lives. Kwok notes the importance of telling stories that have been silenced by the colonizers as they stripped away the historical narrative. Nurturing imagination must include giving a sense of history and knowledge of how the past affects the way we currently live our lives. "The historical imagination aims not to reconstitute the past, but also to release the past so that the present is livable."[xxix] Exploring the past not only gives

46

an understanding of how things came to be; it also gives hope. Exploring the past with a sanctified imagination helps youth to know that similar lives have been lived before God and that God has responded to situations in a variety of ways. Seeing the different ways God has responded to similar situations in the past helps youth to think about how God can work through them to rework their future. "The future is not a grand finale, a classless society, or even a kingdom of God, but more immediate, concrete, and touchable."[xxx] This further distinguishes the task of imagination from that of fantasy. Theological imagination will allow youth to think of concrete ways God can alter their present and future.

Another type of imagination Kwok discusses is diasporic imagination. "Diasporic imagination recognizes the diversity of diasporas and honors the different histories and memories."[xxxi] When speaking of a post-colonial people, this type of imagination is used to bridge different people with different experiences across the diaspora. It is applicable to urban youth, however, because while the youth I speak of may all live and grow in the United States, they cannot all be painted with the same cultural brush. Youth from different contexts need to work together as they discover a new vision for their lives. To fight the feeling of isolation they feel, they ought to be connected and know other youth that are working with similar problems in their context.

These two understandings of imagination work well with the image of the Sankofa bird. It is our diasporic imagination that allows us to glean meaning from an African symbol. The bird's process of moving forward while looking back is in and of itself the use of historical imagination. The past does not control nor define the future, but it does inform it. Using our collective historical and diasporic imagination, world history teaches us that youth want to be an active part of change. They can read an unfair world, imagine a world that is more fair and better, and want to be a part of the process to make that happen. When nurtured, youth will work on their imagined new world. They will do what it takes to create it. When nurtured, young people will put their bodies on the line in order to create this world

47

that they have seen through God's gifted imagination. They will stand in front of tanks, face down dogs and fire hoses, and march in the streets to make things fair. We only need to aid them and allow them to use their sanctified imagination.

Introducing Nia

Whenever I write about youth ministry, I write with particular youth in mind. My writing is about them and for them. Therefore, as part of my autoethnographic method, I use a gestalt to show what my ideas would look when working with a young person. My gestalt's name is Nia. She is a composite of young people with whom I have worked in ministry. As I continue to define the sanctified imagination and how it is nurtured, I will continually return to Nia and ask: How do these theories and ideas affect her life? What does this look like for her? How have we benefitted her? Returning to Nia again and again not only helps us to see how these ideas can be practiced, but also reminds us that the purpose of this work is to change lives—not imaginary theoretical lives, but the real lives of people who struggle with personal hopelessness. My use of this gestalt is not to say that every child in the city lives like Nia. Instead, it is to invite you to put real names and faces and situations from your experiences to this work and to ask the same questions for them as I do for Nia. Nia represents the real people we seek to nurture.

Nia is a fourteen-year-old Black girl living in Small City, USA. Her city used to be one of the premier industrial cities of the United States, but within the last few decades, the industry has declined. Shops and business have left, and revitalization projects have been attempted but have mostly failed. Nia attends the local public high school where 75% of the students fall below the poverty line. Her school district has a 64% graduation rate. Less than 25% of the students show proficiency in math and language arts literacy and 11% of the people in her city over 25 have a college degree. The median income is $35,000—which is $576 below what is needed in this city for a single adult, with no children, to be economically self-sufficient. Nia's family lives below the poverty line.

Nia is active in her local congregation. She attends corporate worship and Sunday school on Sundays as well as Bible Study on Wednesdays. She participates in the choir, dance ministry, drama ministry, and special events in her congregation. She participates mostly because she is fueled by the community there. Nia has also taken part in numerous city-sponsored programs, mostly related to the visual arts. She is a gifted artist. She creates beautiful worlds through her drawings and captures profound realities with her camera. She has amazing visual talent – talent that requires the ability to create new things and see what others do not see.

Nia lives in a crime-ridden neighborhood. She is the oldest of three and often takes care of her younger siblings while her mother works. Her mother works whenever she can, so her work hours are erratic. Nia doesn't like school, and she maintains a "C" average, claiming, "At least I'm not dropping out. I'm going to be a high school graduate!" A couple of months ago, she ran away from home for a month and returned—announcing that she was two months pregnant. Her thoughts about her future are based on basic survival for her and her baby.

Nia's story—like all human stories—is complex and cannot be fully told in a few paragraphs, a few books, or a few volumes. There is joy and struggle. Creativity and conformity. Hope and resignation. Nia's dream is to be an artist, but that seems fanciful to her at this point. She is afraid to imagine that world and instead looks forward to what she believes is her more realistic reality. I do not judge that reality, but I do know that Nia wants to make a different choice but does not believe that she can. It is that relegation to narrowed choices that I judge. How then, does nurturing the sanctified imagination serve her?

Nia has picked up from societal clues that for a person like her to focus on anything other than basic survival is fanciful thinking. However, thoughts of survival are not in conflict with imagination. In fact, sanctified imagination is essential for survival. To harken back to Delores William's terminology, Nia is having a wilderness experience and her best chance of survival is a new vision. Sanctified imagination is a God-given source of survival. Right now, she believes that she is relegated to a particular life because she is a poor, urban, Black, pregnant teen. But like God saw Hagar, God sees Nia and is prepared with a new vision, and God has tasked all those who minister to Nia to aid in nurturing the new vision. Nurturing that new vision happens in a nurturing ecclesiastic community.

Chapter 3

The Nurturing Community

When I was a little girl, I couldn't wait until I was old enough to enter youth group. My two older brothers would always be out with the youth group – skating, retreating, boating, or doing other amazing things. To my ten-year-old eyes, they were doing the coolest things ever! A new youth leader had just been brought on and the group was growing by leaps and bounds. I wanted to be a part of this group so badly. This feeling hit me most strongly on Tuesday nights. Every Tuesday night my family went to prayer meeting. My mom went to the chapel with the adults, my brothers went to the Wisdom Room with the teens, and I went with the other little children to a classroom without a cool name. My envy would rise when the teens would start to sing. The coolest songs would come from the Wisdom Room and float through the air, almost taunting me. These were not the kiddie songs I sang nor were they the old folk hymns that my mother sang. These songs had drumbeats, beatboxing, and dance moves—even the way they praised God was cool! When I finally made it into the Wisdom Room, I thought I had arrived!

Throughout the five years I spent in youth group, the Wisdom Room lived up to its hype. In that room, I found a place where I could challenge and be challenged – a place where it was cool to praise God and hang out with people that praised God. I found out that I didn't really like skating or hiking, but I loved being with the people of God. In that community, I found acceptance.

That community also helped me to find my voice. There were many heated discussions in that Wisdom Room, and I was in the mix of quite a few of them. My first theological debates happened in that room: What does it mean to forgive? How can one be a Christian without being a doormat? How literally can and should one take the Bible? What does it mean to be a Christian lady? Or a Christian gentleman? How important are those gender differences? I was challenged, questioned, and sometimes told I was wrong, but I was never silenced. My voice was encouraged; my passion was ignited. There were some Tuesdays that I was not involved in debate, but instead sat and soaked in the knowledge as people explored answers to questions. The room was named well. I gained a lot of wisdom in that room. That room nurtured the theologian within me way before I knew what a theologian was.

Through that community I also found an extended family. At 16, most youth group members joined other youth from different parishes for the "Christ in Others Retreat" (COR). COR was set up like a nuclear family. There was a mother and father in charge of the weekend. Older volunteers were called aunt, uncle, or big brother/big sister. This was done to intentionally signal the importance of church family, especially in an environment where many of my peers did not grow up in two-parent family homes or, like me, were from families that struggled with some form of dysfunction. COR was meant to model a healthy family where we were to serve each other and hold each other in prayer. Many who went on COR together continued to use these family terms beyond the weekend. I received my first job from one of my COR aunts who approached me simply because she wanted to help me—because that is what Christian family is supposed to do.

After completing COR weekend, many would return to do *Back Up COR*—a service retreat that happened simultaneously. The purpose of this retreat was to serve COR members and prayer for them continuously. Much was asked of us as teenagers and I interpreted that to mean that I could actually *do* much. In that Wisdom Room were song leaders, church council members, and other ministry leaders. Beyond that Wisdom Room was a

53

congregation that took youth seriously. This is the village that raised me. That community was a transformative home that held me close as I grew closer to God and my calling. In that space, my sanctified imagination was nurtured, and it grew exponentially.

The Nurturing Community

Individuals are formed by their interaction with the different communities that raise them. These communities are their neighborhoods, teams, non-profit organizations, schools, and other groups. All communities shape. Therefore, it is important to ask ourselves, "In what ways does my faith community contribute to the shaping of the youth in our communities?" The communities that shape urban youth are as diverse as the population itself. Many laments have been written about the state of urban communities, and I have mentioned some of the concerns earlier in this text. Yet, alongside the lamentations are voices of hope and celebration as people make room to create pockets of urban oases in these communities that positively nurture. Like my youth group experience, there are many congregations that serve as an oasis and nurture the sanctified imagination of youth as youth learn to claim their theological voice.

This chapter will focus on aspects that are foundational for the cultivation of the kind of oasis needed to be a community that nurtures the sanctified imagination. As a practical theologian, I believe that the most powerful setting for fostering this imagination is a faith community. I do not discount the phenomenal secular programs that engage youth in the arts, foster their intellectual community, or focus on the importance of service. These are all important, needed, and capable of fostering the sanctified imagination. However, the best place to focus on seeing one's future with Godly eyes and imagining together what could be created *should be* the local faith community. Faith communities should indeed work with secular organizations but should lead the charge for nurturing this imagination; nurturing the sanctified imagination should be a major goal of local congregations.

I ground my call for placing this work within the local church in an ecclesiology that combines two models of the contemporary church: the intimate community and the diaconal model.[6] The Church as intimate community focuses on the feeling of belonging and support, emphasizing spiritual experiences and relationships with other Christians.[xxxii] This is also a common approach to youth ministry and often expressed in youth ministries that spend much of their time in fellowship. This model of the Church would help provide the community needed for youth to safely find their voice and develop, nurture, and navigate their theological imaginations. But this model needs balance because intimate communities are hard to enter, especially for those who are outsiders, because they either are new or outside of the communal norm for whatever reason. Without balance, the Church can become a community of insider gatherings only concerned with themselves.

Therefore, I place the model of the intimate community in conversation with the diaconal model. Taking its term for the role of a deacon, which is often seen as an office dedicated to service, this model argues that the Church exists to be a servant of the servant Lord. A local congregation that adapts this model sees serving the world as the way they serve God. Their service to the world focuses on the struggle for freedom and justice and serves God by serving the world. This model demands that our ecclesiastical reach extends beyond the walls of a physical church building, implying responsibility for youth even if neither they nor their family have ever darkened our doors.

There is an interesting spin here on the meaning of the Church as servant. The proper service of the Church is to participate in God's liberating activity in the world, exposing conditions of bondage, calling for the conversion of people and corporate structures, prompting prophetic action

---

[6] The work of the church is vast, intricate, and multilayered. There are no models that could encapsulate all that the church is and was meant to be. Yet, these models are useful for emphasis on what aspects are important for a specific goal. The goal here is, of course, the nurturing of the sanctified imagination of urban youth.

on behalf of justice and freedom, and sustaining believers in their solidarity with the poor and their struggle against the powers of evil and injustice. The servant model of the Church helps to overcome the split between the spiritual and the mundane, between concern for evangelization and struggle for justice. Like any singular model, the diaconal model has its weaknesses. There must be a clear understanding of service, which does not mean submission or self-negation. It is also important to keep the diaconal model distinct from social service. Instead it ought to be seen as Christian social justice. Viewing the diaconal model as Christian social justice roots the church in the justice understanding of social holiness and its role in communal sanctification. I am describing an emancipatory ecclesiology.

My notion of emancipatory ecclesiology evolves from Evelyn Parker's concept of emancipatory hope. "Emancipatory hope is expectation that the forms of hegemonic relations—race, class, and gender dominance—will be toppled, and to have emancipatory hope is to acknowledge one's personal agency in God's vision for human equality."[xxxiii] Building upon and borrowing from this definition, emancipatory ecclesiology is the notion that the people of God collectively work towards freedom from oppression and dominance in this day and age. As the Church, we begin by engaging the struggle within our own congregations. We need to incorporate congregational ecclesiologies that remove hierarchies based on race, class, gender or age. If congregations truly seek to be oases that nurture the sanctified imagination so youth can combat personal hopelessness and transform their world, there needs to be an understanding of the systemic oppression that must also be fought against and a rejection of that systemic oppression in the congregation. The congregation also needs to practice a different way. We need more than to fight only for emancipation of others in the world; we ought to be emancipatory within our own ecclesial lives. This involves further grounding emancipatory ecclesiology in a particular understanding of community. The church is not just a community of individuals; it is much deeper than that.

Emancipatory Ecclesiology Calls for the Removal of Dominance

The problems that plague urban communities and lead to personal hopelessness are not just individual or family problems, but problems caused by oppressive systems and structures. In order to be a place that seeks to nurture the sanctified imagination of urban youth, one's community of faith must also be committed to dismantling these oppressive structures.

To further explore the need to work towards the removal of these systemic structures, I turn to Galatians 3:26 – 29, for it addresses the importance of the removal of dominance and oppressive structures that the urban youth I have worked with have had to deal with daily. This passage states, "for in Christ you are all children of God. As many of you as were baptized into Christ have clothed yourselves with Christ. There is no longer Jew or Greek, there is no longer slave or free, there is no longer male and female; for all of you are one in Christ Jesus. And if you belong to Christ, then you are Abraham's offspring, heirs according to the promise."

Some have argued that the declaration of Galatians 3:27 denotes an eschatological ideal that will be accomplished upon Christ's return. Indeed, Paul's eschatology was ever-present as he anticipated Christ's imminent return. Grammatically, however, it is important to note the use of the present tense. "There *is* neither Jew nor Greek, there *is* neither slave nor free, there *is* neither male and female." Additionally, Brad Braxton notes, "With the defection of his converts looming on the horizon it is unlikely that Paul would resort to speculation about the eschatological harmony that Christ would establish. Paul's concern in Galatians 3 is for present harmony."[xxxiv] Our work with youth also necessitates a call for present harmony.

As we strive for present harmony and constantly work for social justice for changes in our present time, Galatians 3:27 is helpful when examined closely. The first question that must be answered: what exactly must "no longer" exist? Many theologians talk of a removal of distinctions. This creates a quandary because gender and racial differences still exist among the baptized—it cannot *not* exist. Moreover, there should be no desire for these identities not to exist. Too often people deal with diversity by simply saying they don't see it. It is common to say, "I don't see color." Yet, what that really means is that a person is not being fully seen. Racial difference is not a hindrance that needs to be overcome, but a rich God-given diversity that needs to be embraced. So, if this verse speaks of the removal of difference, then the verse must be read symbolically. However, along with Brad Braxton, I believe that as we look at Paul's pairings, we ought not to see these espousing "the obliteration of difference, but rather the obliteration of dominance."[xxxv] One should not be forced to give up distinctions that make them uniquely them. Braxton continues:

> Even 'in Christ' there is still human difference. The
> dominance of one over the other based on these
> differences is the reality that is abolished! In Christ,
> Jews are not to be dominant over Gentiles; free
> persons are not to be dominant over slaves; men are
> not to be dominant over women.[xxxvi]

Differences ought to be embraced; oppression based upon those differences ought to be abolished. A culture where one is made to feel inferior because they do not live up to the hegemonic norm ought to be abolished. And any policies based on perpetuating a racist, sexist, and classist system ought to be abolished.

The first of the three pairs refers to racial dominance, "there is no longer Jew or Greek," is the one that many note as fitting more within in the context of the letter to the Galatians, for the bulk of letter speaks to not being coerced by racial domination. Braxton argues:

> By proclaiming a gospel of uncircumcision Paul was helping in some
> limited way to establish a Gentile Christian identity. The Gentile
> believer was a Christian, but was not a Jewish Christian. Paul was
> thus encouraging the Gentile believers to say 'no' to the dominant
> ideology of the Judaizers, but he does not appear to be encouraging
> them to say 'yes' to Gentile culture *per se*.[xxxvii]

Paul is encouraging them to find their own unique identity. They were not Jewish, so they could not be Jewish Christians. Yet, because they were Christians, they could not completely embrace a Gentile culture that was not Christian. They then had to explore to create something new in order to be both Gentile and Christian. This is part of the task of theological imagination—realizing that the current situation does not fit into current paradigms and prayerfully creating a new paradigm.

The second of three pairs refers to the removal of economic oppression. "There is neither slave nor free." Because they are written as three parallel pairs, one may be tempted to view them all in the same way. However, while there are certainly parallels, these pairs point to important differences. Viewing this passage as a call for the removal of difference, the argument is founded on the idea that Greek and Jew can exist and partake in the table of Christ together without one having to become the other. "By contrast, in the case of the slave/free distinction, 'in Christ' the difference is abolished, because the slave knows freedom in Christ."[xxxviii] Working for social justice does not allow us to simply accept the poverty of others and ask them to accept their poverty and simply worship Christ through it. We ought to seek to eradicate both economic oppression and the root of poverty itself. "Actually, Paul's entire argument is based on the possibility of moving from a state of slavery to freedom; those who were once slaves can be set free."[xxxix] Certainly, there is a freedom within Christ.

"While it is true that Paul emphasizes his metaphorical usage here, one cannot ignore that, against the backdrop of a Roman society and economy based on slavery, the social and legal implications of this language would resonate loudly."[xl] This language resonates loudly within the society of the United States as well. Within many congregations, the answer to post-slavery economic oppression is to create a group to "get a piece of the pie" and become economically privileged. So often, this transfers the power between players within economic oppression; it does not eliminate it. We ought not be satisfied simply with teaching people how to gain economic prosperity in a way that they too may become oppressors. My contention is not with removing individuals from poverty. My contention is with the idea that that is enough.

We must embrace emancipatory practices that seek to fight against institutions that create the slave/free dichotomy in any form. Often, the argument against removing economic oppression lies in the sharing of the economic prosperity of the privileged. Many do not disagree with raising the wealth of others as long as it does not result in decreasing their own wealth. Emancipatory practices recognizes that we ought not see our neighbor as competition. Instead, "[my] freedom begins when my real neighbor—especially the poor, the weak, the needy—becomes the motive of my actions, when individualism is overcome by community."[xli] Emancipatory practices can only exist within community—a community where people bear each other's burdens and an individual constantly seeks the benefit of another.

The final pair seeks to remove gender dominance. Unlike the other pairings, this pairing does not state there is no longer male *nor* female. Instead, it states, "there is no longer male *and* female." "This is in order to take over the exact wording of Gen 1:27 from its formulation in the Septuagint, thus emphasizing the 'new creation' which has taken shape in Christ."[xlii] With this third pair, Paul reminds us that God created both male and female. Both male and female have the *Imago Dei* within. Emancipatory practices welcome women in whatever capacity God calls them to serve, for one human cannot put limits on another human. To do that is to reverse the freedom God gives.

This biblical text serves as a theological foundation for ubuntu as a foundation for urban ecclesiology. Many of the youth I served existed in places where these oppressive forces came together to cause a feeling of personal hopelessness—if the youth believes the messages being sent. The world approaches them with an intersection of oppression, but God approaches them with an intersection of freedom. With the freedom encountered with Christ, youth should be armed with ways to oppose the things that threaten to silence or entrap them and be encouraged to find an identity different from the one being pushed upon them.

Embracing Ubuntu as an Ecclesiological Identity

Ubuntu—pronounced oo-BOON-too—derives from Sub-Saharan African cultures and a group of languages known as Bantu. The meaning of ubuntu is revealed in the African proverb, "I am because we are." It is also expressed through a proverb I grew up hearing in the Caribbean, "All of we is one." This concept recognizes that if we are truly living in community, my humanity depends on your humanity. I could not truly be *me* without you and you could not truly be *you* without me. We are not in competition with others or focused on the rugged individualism that is within the DNA of Western society. For those that pride themselves on independence, the idea of true interdependence may sound restricting. For those who see true adulthood as a period of self-sufficiency and believe youth should be trained to be ready to stand on their own, the idea of interdependence may seem akin to codependence. "Ubuntu, however, is about symbiotic and cooperative relationships."[xliii] These relationships are not codependent nor destructive, but healthy and mutually beneficial.

While this may be a jarring concept for those steeped only within Western culture, this is not a foreign concept to Christians. To the contrary, it is essential to Christian identity and the formation of Church. Christians are Christians because of relationship. First there is a relationship with Jesus Christ—who is understood within his own Trinitarian relationship. Christians are also called to be in relationship with each other as through various passages with the biblical text. One such example comes from Paul's letter to the Romans. "For as in one body we have many members, and not all the members have the same function, so we, who are many, are one body in Christ, and individually we are members one of another" (Romans 12:4 &5). This section of Paul's letter to the Romans is a call to practice ubuntu. Paul notes the necessity of the individual living into their own calling, for the body functions best when all the body parts do what they were created to do. Yet, we are called to recognize that not only are we part of Christ, but we are also one in Christ. Meaning as members of this body of Christ, we are part of each other. That is a call to ubuntu.

The call to ubuntu is also expressed in the modern gospel song *I Need You to Survive*:

I need you

You need me

We're all a part of God's body

Stand with me

Agree with me

We're all a part of God's body

It is his will that every need be supplied

You are important to me

I need you to survive.[xliv]

This expression of Christian unity understands the need for ubuntu as foundational to ecclesiology. For us to truly be the church—part of God's body—we need to recognize our interdependence. We need each other. It is not merely that life is easier with help from others or that we get further with others or that others help us to thrive. Ubuntu is more fundamental and crucial than that. We need each other to survive. We require the existence and thriving of others in order for we ourselves to exist and thrive as individuals and as a community. That is what being a part of God's body calls us to recognize. Communal survival is a benefit of ubuntu and leads to its emancipatory nature. Ubuntu is an emancipatory concept, for it cannot exist within a congregation or system that is racist, sexist, classist, or oppressive in any way. For oppressing the other is also oppressing ourselves and dehumanizing the other dehumanizes ourselves.

Recognizing that our interdependence means we rely on each other, it is important that this vision includes youth as equal members of a congregation. This community includes children and youth as full members of Christ's body. Part of what made my youth ministry experience so powerful was the recognition that we were not the "church of the future" –

we were full members of the church in the present with the same access to the Holy Spirit that adults had, and we were expected to act as such.

Revisiting Nia: Emancipatory Ecclesiology, Ubuntu, and the Sanctified Imagination

Let us return to our gestalt, Nia, and imagine her being a part of a congregation practicing an emancipatory ecclesiology. What does that look like? Because Nia is a part of an intimate community, she feels at home. She is regularly in a space that tells her that she is accepted. She is encouraged to be her true self and seek an authenticity that adolescents often crave. This also means that people are being their authentic true selves with her, and she is trusted with this kind of vulnerability. This requires a great deal of trust. If the trust is broken—because she and the people around her are humans that make mistakes—then different ways of repairing the damage will be explored. Part of intimay and being our true selves is the recognition that we are flawed individuals. So, Nia does not get shunned or shut out when she makes a mistake; she is, instead, encouraged to grow. Nia lives in a world where mistakes have dire consequences that brand for life. Black and Latinx urban youth are sometimes policed in a way that other youths are not. School fights that might be dealt with by teachers or principals in other contexts are dealt with by school police and truancy officers in Nia's context. Nia may know someone who has a criminal record for drugs. Major mistakes that may be seen as youthful indiscretion in other communities have lifelong consequences in Nia's world. An intimate community will be there to listen to Nia's confusions and frustrations about her world along with concerns of identity that all adolescents face. And if she is one of those that makes a "big" mistake, Nia will benefit from a community that will know her enough to hopefully know if she is going down a dangerous path, try to intervene, and be there to pick her up.

Being a part of a community that is also focused on serving God by serving the world through working for freedom and justice, helps Nia's focus not to be too inward and individualized. Yes, the work is meant to benefit the world that Nia is in, but it will also call Nia to look outside of herself at a time where youth can be self-absorbed. Because she is in a congregation that works for the betterment of the world, Nia may be more aware of what is happening in the world. She may not only serve at soup kitchens but be aware of some of the reasons that hunger is a prevalent problem in her community. She will be able to communicate the problem with school policing. Getting Nia to think outside of herself also lets her know that many of the problems that she faces are not her fault. The intimate community then surrounds her when she comes to the difficult realization that she may be categorized as at-risk through no fault of her own but based on the city she was born in, the school system that she is legally obligated to be a part of, and other decisions that were made for her. And the justice-oriented community reminds her just because things are currently this way does not mean that it must stay this way. With their communal imagination, Nia's congregation begins to think of ways to change the problematic structures that will also change things for Nia, her family, and her friends.

Within a congregation that seeks to embrace ubuntu, Nia has a voice. Her voice is not only encouraged but sought after because her voice is an integral part of the community's well-being. She understands that she does not have the same experience as older members in the congregation, but she sees herself as having the same value. She can put her voice into the conversation, and have it taken seriously. Having a voice in her church community gives Nia the courage and ability to use her voice in other settings because she has been made aware of its power and importance.

With ubuntu as an ecclesiological starting point, Nia is not only part of a church family that surrounds her, but she is part of a community that needs her. To be needed is a powerful thing. Once one is needed, one also must rise to the occasion. There are expectations placed on Nia and Nia is expected to meet them. Does this mean that she will always do what is expected of her? No. No one does. But this does mean that she knows that there are others who believe that she is able to do wonderful things, and that belief alone can often spur someone to move beyond the limitations other sections of society place on them because of their race, class, and gender? Nia will thrive in a place that tells her that all these stories of dominance are lies. Because Nia is being nurtured in a theology that is freeing, she will know that these limitations placed on her are not of God. Being a congregation that fights against injustice requires acquiring knowledge about the causes of these problems and studying other contexts that have combatted these problems in various ways. This process inherently nurtures the diasporic imagination and widens the notion of ubuntu. Nia will learn that not only are the people in her small oasis of a community reliant on each other, but the wider diaspora of communities that are similar to hers are in this together and learn from each other.

There are times that trying to achieve this kind of ecclesiastical identity may seem like a fantasy. However, as a congregation strives for this mark, the communal historic imagination will also be nurtured. Nia and her church community will continuously remember that God has worked wonders in the past. People from oppressed communities throughout time have found churches to be freeing places—an oasis where their voices are heard and nurtured. And because of the confidence and strength they gained in their intimate communities, they were empowered to bring their voices of change outside of the walls of their congregation. People of God have changed their communities before, so it is not naive to believe that the people of God can make changes again.

With Nia in this community, other questions arise. In what concrete ways does this community surround Nia and allow Nia and other youth to surround them? Are there particular ways that Nia and her nurturing community can enact their historical and diasporic imagination as they nurture each other's sanctified imagination? Once the community is formed, what is at least one place they go from here? The next chapter looks at the role of mentoring as one particular way the nurturing community can nurture their communal imagination.

Chapter 4

The Nurturing Community as Intergenerational Mentoring Community

An interesting thing was happening while I was a youth in that Wisdom Room. A significant portion of the group was getting older, and the congregation had no young adult ministry. So, I found myself in the Wisdom Room with about a quarter of the group members being adults in their 20s. The youth leader used this opportunity to form a cadre of young leaders. They were to serve as organizers and teachers, but many of them were new themselves to the faith. Partnered with a group of people who (like me) had eagerly counted down to when they could join youth group, these youth leaders found themselves not always leading, but at times walking beside or even being led. What developed in that room were beautiful and life-giving intergenerational relationships and reciprocal mentoring.

There were some problems; it seemed like the main qualification for being a leader was being older, more so than a sense of call. Lines were blurred as people who were not peers often acted like peers and this led to a variety of problems. The youth leader was simply trying to make the best out of the situation he had—it really happened by accident. But as I think about a communal paradigm for nurturing the sanctified imagination, I think back to the Wisdom Room and wonder what greater things could have happened if intergenerational relationships and reciprocal mentoring had been done on purpose.

The mentoring that took place in that Wisdom Room was multifaceted. As youth we were in search of and in need of mentoring. We were passionate, but naïve, inexperienced, and partially informed. We needed guidance and received it not only in large group settings, but through smaller one-on-one mentoring relationships. But in addition to this type of traditional mentoring, we also got to mentor some of the older individuals. As a youth trained in Catholic schools and years of catechism, I've had many conversations about living out one's faith. This could be a helpful insight for an adult new to the faith. Through these intergenerational relationships we learned that we could share knowledge on a variety of things. There was also space for bi-directional mentoring as we shared our knowledge with each other. Reflecting on my experiences leads me to think of three types of mentoring that nurturing communities ought to embrace in order to nurture the sanctified imagination of youth: traditional top-down mentoring, reverse mentoring (bottom-up), and bi-directional mentoring where youth and adults work together on a project and mentor each other.

Understanding Mentoring

The word "mentor" comes from the character of the same name in Homer's *The Odyssey*. Odysseus, king of Ithaca, leaves home to fight in the Trojan War and entrusts the care of his household to Mentor, who serves as teacher and overseer of Odysseus' young son, Telemachus. Even after years of fighting in the war, Odysseus does not return home immediately, but instead finds himself condemned to wander vainly and be kept from his family for another ten years. Once it appears that Odysseus is not returning home, Odysseus's home is overrun by suitors vying for Odysseus's wife, Penelope. The suitors disrespect Penelope, Telemachus, and their home as they take advantage of Odysseus's absence. In time, a now-grown Telemachus, wanting to stop the problematic behavior that has taken over his home, ventures in search of his father. Athena, goddess of war and patroness of the arts and industry, assumes the form of Mentor and accompanies Telemachus on his quest. As Mentor, she guides and protects him. They return, having not found Odysseus, and discover that the situation at home has gotten even worse. Eventually, Odysseus returns home. Father and son reunite and, along with Athena, fight the suitors and cast down the would-be usurpers of Odysseus's throne and Telemachus's birthright.

I share this etymology because it shows some of the multifaceted sides of mentoring. All three types of mentoring are present in the etymology of this term. When Odysseus leaves, he entrusts the most important thing in his life—his family—to Mentor. This is not a role that is taken lightly, and this is not a term that can be ascribed to just anyone. A mentor is someone that can be trusted with the things one holds most dear, like one's dreams, hopes, and desires for themselves and the world around them. A mentor teaches, guides, and protects. When Telemachus, looking around his world and seeing that something is not right, goes on a quest to make it right, Mentor does not tell Telemachus to simply accept the wrong behavior of his elders, but encourages him to make things right, suggests ways this can be done, and journeys with him in his search. And at this point, the mentor has a divine presence—a recognition that something larger is happening here beyond the two people in the relationship. When they return from this quest and the time comes to fight for what is right, Mentor/Athena fights right alongside Telemachus and his father. Telemachus has the desire for change, justice, and fairness. Mentor nurtures and shapes that by journeying and fighting beside young Telemachus with the power of the divine.

The older mentor does not always lead, but often walks beside and struggles along with the younger charge. This opens up a relationship of mutual sharing, teaching, and changing. May we seek to nurture the youthful search for fairness by creating this kind of cross-generational relationship. This type of relationship values the experiences of both parties and believes that both parties have something to learn from the other. Yet before Telemachus is able to initiate a trip with Mentor/Athena or fight beside this mentor, he first has to be cared for and nurtured by Mentor.

The Mentoring Community

The Church as a mentoring community serves roles that are as multifaceted as the etymology of the word, and it is grounded in the notion of the divine presence that takes place in mentoring. While the mentor is not the divine in human form like Athena, there is a divine presence that manifests in mentoring relationships when people seek to use their sanctified imagination together. A community committed to God and each other is also empowered by the Holy Spirit. Additionally, loving God allows us to know God better, and in our understanding of a sanctified imagination in viewing sanctification as perfect love, we recognize that one cannot love God without loving neighbor. Loving neighbor and living into that love in a mentoring relationship also allows us to know God better. The sanctified mentoring relationship, then, becomes a placeholder for Divine presence with God's presence in our mentoring relationship. The mentoring also strengthens the resolve to participate in the reign of God as we also see sanctification as social holiness. We do not live out our faith in isolation; we live out our faith with each other and, when done well, a mentoring relationship better helps both parties live out their faith and fortifies their sanctified imagination.

Adolescents present particular needs that would be served well by healthy mentoring communities. After infancy, adolescence is the period in which there is the most physical and mental growth. Puberty manifests not only in changing bodies but also in rapid brain development. Adolescents have great ability to learn new things and make connections between the new things they are learning and the old things they already knew. They are able to synthesize vast amounts of information. Their brains are shaping and forming in ways that they will carry with them for the rest of their lives. This is also a period of identity formation. This does not mean that one's identity is set during adolescence; identity continues to shift. While there are consistent themes of adolescent development that run through different contexts, adolescent development is also contextual. Therefore, placing adolescents in healthy contexts has a positive effect on their identity formation. This can also be a period of searching for self where adolescents play with different personas and see what feels genuine. This is a prime time for a mentor to note something positive seen in the youth that can be further developed.

As we explore the effect of context on how adolescents develop, it is important to explore different dimensions. In their 1998 publication reflecting on ethnographic study, Michelle Fine and Lois Weis present three common material bases that shaped their participants' sense of self and others: the body, the economy/economic opportunities, and the state/social policies.[xlv] Fine and Weis do not present these as affecting development in the same way for everyone, but recognize the nuances in peoples' experiences. These three foci are often not present in an older presentation of how adolescents develop, yet these areas are particularly relevant to the urban youth with whom I have worked. The youth with whom I have worked were aware of how these three foci affected their lives. They frequently discussed how their embodied identities (with regard to race and gender, the economic reality of their parents, and the help their families are able to get and not get because of their economic reality) affects the way they view the world and their place in it. And they craved relationships with adults that would help them navigate these choppy waters; healthy relationships are key to healthy adolescent development.

"Our relationships are the sites in which we negotiate not only our individuated sense of self, as both autonomous and connected to others, but also our identities in relation to macro social categories such as gender, race, and class."[xlvi] Development occurs through relationship and mentoring relationships. With mentoring relationships being necessary to adolescent development, what better community for youth to consider a mentoring community than the congregation with which they worship?

As mentoring communities, congregations can work with youth as partners and teachers as they navigate the world around them. My idea for a mentoring community is partially based on the work of Sharon Daloz Parks.

Parks links the concepts of faith, development, imagination, and mentoring. Parks' work is rooted in a particular understanding of faith. Parks does not seek to understand the faith of young people merely as a system of beliefs. Instead, she focuses on how young adults make meaning of and from their lives:

> This mode of making meaning includes (1) becoming critically aware of one's own composing of reality, (2) self-consciously participating in an ongoing dialogue toward truth, and (3) cultivating a capacity to respond—to act—in ways that are satisfying and just.[xlvii]

This understanding of making meaning is a great challenge for all those that work with youth. We seek to prepare youth who will be able to adopt this paradigm of meaning-making more readily as a young adult. Corporate theological imagination asks youth to become aware of their own reality as they seek to transform it, and this is essential to young people as they try to find their footing in this world and live into an all-encompassing faith that helps them make meaning of their lives. When faith is thought of as a way of making meaning, faith is then seen as all-encompassing. It is a faith is that transcends us and undergirds our existence.[xlviii] It is foundational to the entire life of a person—further making congregations ideal mentoring communities.

"A mentoring community offers hospitality to the potential of the emerging self, and it offers access to worthy dreams of self and world."[xlix] This role is an extension to the church's role as a nurturing community. Although a nurturing community is often associated with a traditional form of mentoring where the adult mentors and the youth learn, urban youth are bombarded with groups masquerading as mentoring communities. Gangs, neighborhood cliques, and consumer culture as a whole try to seduce these youth into their world with the promise of complete acceptance. Yet, all of them require digesting a very particular ideology that must not be questioned. It is important that local congregations do not appear simply as another group claiming to give community, but only practice true acceptance when all ideologies are accepted. Instead, congregations ministering to these youth are challenged to create communities where teens can challenge, disagree, grow, try, fail, fall, and be caught. Those that have fallen in ways that have severed them from this community can be welcomed again with open arms.

Mentoring does not only happen when the older mentors the young; sometimes the young mentors the old. When this is done formally, it is called reverse mentoring, a practice that began in the business world. Business leaders looking to stay current with e-business trends and to use growing technologies to their advantage began asking for guidance from their younger colleagues. While reverse mentoring, also called bottom-up mentoring, has probably informally existed for as long as different generations have shared the same workplace, the formalization of it in business started in 1999 with Jack Welch, former CEO of General Electric Corp. Welch got the idea from a colleague when he was struggling with Internet skills. He received help from a younger person within the company that had knowledge of the technology. Once helped, he developed a program where over 600 managers took part in a reverse mentoring program.[1]

During my research on reverse mentoring, a consistent theme constantly rose to the surface: Both the mentee *and* the mentor stated that they got a lot out of the relationship. The mentors (the younger ones) received various types of career and life advice while the mentees learned particular aspects of the technology. I found a similar sentiment in a meeting with adults trying to set up an "adopt a grandparent" program with a nearby senior citizen housing facility. We thought we would begin by asking people to come together to share and teach their gifts. Ideas started pouring in. Senior citizens could teach cooking, knitting, basic house repairs, crafting, the list went on and on. "What can the teens teach?" I asked. There was a pause until someone said, "Computers, I guess." But, surely, young people know more that how to navigate the latest technology. The limited view of the gifts young people have to offer can make reverse mentoring much less powerful than it can be.

In his book, *Reverse Mentoring: How Young Leaders Can Transform the Church and Why We Should let Them*, Earl Creps quotes a friend who sums up reverse mentoring. The essence of reverse mentoring is "young people, who help older people, learn young stuff."[li] This begs the question, what is "young stuff?" Besides being a technology native (assuming one's family has the finances for one to be a technology native), what do these youth have to offer? When I asked this question in a room full of youth ministers, certain themes kept being repeated: energy, a desire for fairness, a belief that things can change, a hopeful naïveté. To that list I add, imagination. As I have argued, I believe that imagination is something innate in children but repressed by school systems. Therefore, part of nurturing the sanctified imagination is protecting the imagination from being squelched. This happens when young people are mentored by adults, when they are asked to mentor adults, and when this comes together in a bidirectional intergenerational mentoring relationship. Reciprocal mentoring and intergenerational relationships are a place where youth can express these thoughts and have them nurtured.

I propose a mentoring community that includes cross-generational partnership and reciprocal mentoring. This type of partnership values the experiences of both parties and believes that both parties have something to learn from the other. We recognize that adults have more experience and can be more of a guide, but we also recognize that more experience also means more time being silenced. We all need to be freed, and since youth have spent less time on earth being silenced, that youthful outlook of "things can be fair" needs to rub off on some adults.

Cross-generational partnerships and reciprocal mentoring also allows us to truly see each other. Top-down teaching relationships means that the students know what the teacher thinks, and the teacher may know what outspoken students think, but so many students are more concerned about saying the right answer that they don't give the real answer. We don't always know what they think and why they think it. Reciprocal mentoring allows us to really know each other and shape each other's lives.

Ubuntu with a Multigenerational Dimension

While we recognize that youth should be seen as today's Christians in full connection with the Church and that all the members of the Church, regardless of age, are equal in value and voice, they are not equal in maturity, experience, or ability to process. Age contributes to this dissimilarity. The work of nurturing the sanctified imagination is multigenerational work. Therefore, the community that chooses to nurture the sanctified imagination of youth must possess a developmentally appropriate approach. In his work on the stage developmental theory of faith, James Fowler termed the type of the faith often found within the teen years as "synthetic-conventional faith." Synthetic refers to the adolescent's new cognitive ability to pull things together. The adolescent is now able to pull together different visions of self, values, and beliefs. It is paired with conventional for two reasons

> It is a synthesis of belief and value elements that are
> derived from one's significant others . . . [and] . . .
> the beliefs, values, and stories that compose a
> person's faith outlook and support his or her
> emerging identity [that] are not yet objectified for
> critical reflection by that person.[lii]

At this age, a young person's world expands beyond family as a number of different areas (school, work, peers, sports, clubs, church, etc.) clamor for their attention. So, they simultaneously branch out and take on the values of their significant others. They claim the values of the people they value and create a unique and personal fusion, but the elements themselves are conventional. It is also conventional because this personal fusion has not yet been critically reflected upon. As the name explains, at this stage, youth are synthesizing different conventional norms.

Now that adolescents are able to hold different views, they are able to cognitively imagine different lifestyles for themselves and the possibility that God may want different for them. They are able to view different aspects of God. They are able to synthesize different views, balance the voices of others, Scripture, worship, sermons, etc. and bring them all together to a place where they can hear God. However, providing a healthy community for them to explore this stage is crucial, for it is also a stage where they internalize the expectation of people with whom they have serious relations and seek to conform to those expectations. They do not yet have a sure enough understanding of their own sense of self and sense of agency in order to try to create and maintain an independent viewpoint.[liii] It is a paradoxical stage where youth test their independent thought by mimicking those of their family unit or test their independence from their parents by conforming to the code of their peers. And with this stage comes two particular dangers: "The expectations and evaluations of others can be so compellingly internalized (and sacralized) that later autonomy of judgment and action can be jeopardized; or interpersonal betrayals can give rise either to nihilistic despair about a personal principle of ultimate being or to a compensatory intimacy with God unrelated to mundane relations."[liv] For better or worse, youth are shaped by their environments. If it is an environment that encourages them to think critically and teaches them how to use their newfound cognitive ability to synthesize information and come up with different ideas or conclusions—they may blossom. However, if it is an environment that continuously tells them what to think and is extremely rigid about their education, persona, and decision-making abilities, then they may never leave this stage and it may be harder to later learn critical thinking. It is essential, therefore, that congregations provide the former community and not the latter. For this reason, the model of the local church as an intimate community and embracing ubuntu as an ecclesial identity is helpful. It focuses on the promotion of relationships and the cultivating of spiritual experiences. And in many ways healthy relationships are the vehicles for spiritual experiences, the theological formation, and the nurturing of imagination.

In bidirectional mentoring relationships, it is important to remember the role of authority. "A person's feelings continue to be shaped by assumed Authority until the day there is a yearning (or the absolute necessity) to explore and test trust for oneself."[lv] At certain points in our lives authority is needed (though to the degree that law enforcement and the government are authorities, they are always needed), but authority should be given based on a knowledge and trust that one is being led to greater understanding and eventual independence to become one's own authority on some level—that is part of what theological imagination and critical thinking seeks to do.

In this paradigm, the congregation is called to partner with young people and create a shared authority, an inner-dependence of sorts. They are not peers, but they do recognize their shared need for each other as they embrace the concept of ubuntu.

> In contrast to the common associations we make with independence or autonomy, inner-dependencies is not intended to connote standing all by oneself. Rather, the developmental movement into inner-dependence occurs when one is able self-consciously to include the self within the arena of authority.[lvi]

All youth may not be ready cognitively to make this move, but some will be, and those that are not ready should know that it is an acceptable and even expected move to make. However, this notion of inner-dependence and shared authority in relation to teens needs to be a notion not only accepted by them, but by adult leaders in their communities. Congregations may fear nurturing teens' imaginations; it takes power away from congregational leaders. Those that partner with youth to foster imagination need to be ready for their role of authority to change. This is the move from complete authority figure to a mentor facilitating a mentoring community.

Mentoring Nia

In a nurturing community that recognizes the power within youth, there would be many opportunities for youth to be in ministry with people of different generations. Nia may find herself naturally gravitating towards an adult with whom she has something in common. Youth leaders should pay special attention to this, assess whether the adult would make a good mentor for the youth, and approach the adult about mentoring the youth in a more formal way. For the purpose of this gestalt, let's call the mentor Pam or, as Nia would call her, Ms. Pam.

Although there may be several in Nia's congregation that would make wonderful mentors, the first obstacle is often convincing potential mentors of the knowledge they contain—a knowledge that is not only worthy of sharing, but one that ought to be shared for the betterment of another. Teens are not the only ones who believe the lies that place limitations on them. Adults can be hesitant to see themselves as capable of being mentors. Ms. Pam may feel like she has little tidbits to share here and there, but not necessarily have the wherewithal to be a long-term mentor that gives faithful and spiritual guidance—even though she is more than capable. I have found that there are a few ways to quell this nervousness in adults.

First, note what you see in this adult and why you are approaching them. If Nia is already forming a healthy bond with Ms. Pam, this would be the first point. Youth crave authenticity; therefore, if a youth is drawn to an adult, there is something authentic they are seeing within that adult and something that they feel they can learn from that person. It would also let Pam know that Nia likes her—and that says something. Ms. Pam would also benefit from hearing what qualities I, as the youth leader, feel would benefit both the adult and the youth in the mentoring relationship. Finally, I would offer support. Since healthy mentorships are beneficial and unhealthy mentorships are detrimental to youth development, ongoing conversations and training with Ms. Pam would give some structure to the organic relationship that was formed between Nia and Ms. Pam and allow the youth leader to assess the healthiness and compatibility of this relationship. This does not mean that the youth leader must actively manage or oversee every adult/youth relationship in the congregation but be mindful and aware of it and be in casual conversation with Ms. Pam from time to time and offer insights if needed. As Nia and Ms. Pam get closer and form a deeper healthy relationship, the youth leader will slowly remove themselves from the situation. If the relationship seems unhealthy, however, the youth leader should intervene, call out unhealthy behavior, and try to stop it.

It may also be possible that Nia does not naturally gravitate to anyone. In that case, leaders should approach an adult with the same goals of finding Nia an appropriate healthy relationship stating why the youth leader thinks it would be a good match, what healthy qualities the youth leader thinks the adult has, and the offer of support for the mentor. For these pairings a more formal mentoring program with group activities would be beneficial and a great way to build relationships.

Because of power dynamics, I would not encourage an adult to approach a youth and ask them directly to be in a mentoring relationship, nor would I state that an adult initiated a pairing. It may be difficult for Nia to say that she is uncomfortable for whatever reason with an adult if it is clear that the adult desires this relationship. I may mention that Ms. Pam sees something special in her and suggest that they get to know each other, but I would not be the matchmaker on Ms. Pam's behalf.

While I think it is important for children to have healthy role models of all genders, when possible, I prefer same-gender mentoring. As Nia is trying to figure out her identity as a young woman, the more examples of healthy manifestations of womanhood she is exposed to, the better. This will further the notion of not trying to fit into a cookie-cutter image of what others think one ought to be. Recognizing that there are different models for being a woman of faith would be extremely beneficial for Nia. It is also beneficial to assess the mentoring relationship from time to time to see if the relationship is still a fit. Relationships can cease to be a fit for perfectly healthy reasons like just growing apart from each other, outgrowing the relationship because interests have changed, or schedule changes that make it difficult to see each other often.

As the mentoring relationship gets formalized, the youth minister should check in with the mentor often just to see how it is going. There might also be some opportunity for mentoring activities or studies that would be an intergenerational gathering, where all adults and youth that are participating in this formal mentoring program are brought together for fellowship, service, or study. This also creates an intergenerational environment where Nia is not only in communication with her own mentor but with other adults from the faith community as well. In these gatherings, it is important to remember that youth and adults should be given a chance to teach each other.

In mentoring relationships that are part of mentoring programs overseen by youth leaders, there are two levels of activities. There are the activities that leaders organize and then the activities that mentors and mentees organically decide on their own. Group organized activities are a great way for adults and youth who do not know each other to get to know each other in a less awkward way. These activities are a great way to model bi-directional mentoring. These activities would vary by context but would share a few key basics.

First, these activities would give equal voice to youth and adults and not allow voices to be dismissed because of age. Sometimes in intergenerational gatherings, different opinions are dismissed because they are told that they lack experience (they are too young to understand) or they are out of touch (too old to understand). What is really being said is, "You don't have the same experience that I have." While this is a valid point for both age groups, it can be expressed without being dismissive. Group discussions would give everyone space to share their experiences and show how their experiences have framed their opinions and value each other's experiences.

These activities should model healthy boundaries. Adults and youth are not peers. While it is developmentally appropriate for youth to challenge authority, it must be realized that adult leadership is still needed and the difference in age must still be acknowledged. It is inappropriate for adults and children to act like peers. Some distance must be created. This is why Nia calls Pam "Ms. Pam." This is a sign of respect for an adult that is not your peer.

Both youth and adults should be given the opportunity to lead and teach. Whether it is informal discussions, intergenerational Bible studies, worship services, or any planned activity with youth and adults, we should always be modeling bi-directional mentoring, teaching, and learning. Youth have gifts, wisdom, and insights to share. There should be no doubt that their voices are welcomed. While this is not an exhaustive list of things that we ought to be mindful of when forming bi-directional mentoring programs, these are some basics that would constantly remind Nia and Ms. Pam that they have a lot to learn from each other, and together both of their sanctified imaginations would be nurtured by this experience.

Bi-directional mentoring and intergenerational relationships can have great power for nurturing the communal imagination. The variety of experiences, knowledge, and viewpoints present make it fertile ground for nurturing the historical and diasporic imagination. With voices from different generations being shared and listened to equally, stories of God's movement in other spaces and times can cultivate a variety of possibilities and new vision. This, in many ways, in the task of Christian Education— cultivating new ways of seeing and knowing so that everyone can be freed to be the person God created them to be. In the next chapter, we explore particular approaches to Christian Education that aid in the nurturing of the sanctified imagination.

Chapter 5

Imagining Together: Christian Education as Sharing Wisdom

In the 23rd Chapter of her memoir *I Know Why the Caged Bird Sings*, Maya Angelou recounts her eighth-grade graduation from the Negro grammar school in segregated Stamps, Arkansas. She remembers a day filled with excitement and anticipation where the graduates were treated like royalty. For many in her small community, this is one of the few occasions calling for new clothes—for graduating children and their parents. The entire community was excited; her minister had preached on the importance of graduation the Sunday before. This was a proud time for the Negro community of Stamps. Angelou was beaming in the yellow dress her grandmother had labored over. Awarded one of the top places in the class, she would be one of the first called in the ceremony. She rehearsed the exercises with her best friend until they were exhausted. She was excited and anticipated a magical day.

The commencement speaker was a White elected official who began by speaking about the wonderful changes the children of Stamps were about to see. Due to his efforts, he boasted, The Central School (the White School) was going to have a well-known artist from Little Rock come to teach the art class. They were also getting upgrades in their science laboratory that included new microscopes and other updated equipment. He went on to praise the students in his presence by reminding them that they had produced one of the best basketball players at Fisk and a first-line football tackler at Arkansas Agricultural and Mechanical College. The speaker promised that if the parents voted for him, their children would have the privilege of going to the only colored school with a paved playing field in that part of Arkansas. He also promised to get some new equipment for the home economics building and the workshop.

The contrast of expectations and preparations hit Angelou hard, for she had once again received society's message:

> The white kids were going to have a chance to become
> Galileos and Madame Curies and Edisons and Gauguins,
> and our boys (the girls weren't even in on it) would try to be
> Jesse Oweneses and Joe Louises. Owens and the Brown Bomber
> were great heroes in our world but what school official in the
> white-goddom of Little Rock had the right to decide that those
> two men must be our only heroes?[lvii]

Angelou heard the message that many Black youth still hear today. Once again, she was reminded that the greater society placed a cap on her potential and success – and that, only when they even recognized her at all. "We were maids and farmers, handymen and washer-women, and anything higher that we aspired to was farcical and presumptuous."[lviii] Angelou was not the only one weighed down by the gravity of this lesson. She notes that the mood of the entire crowd changed. The crowd that had piled into the seats with laughter and peppered the principal's opening speech with Amens and resounding response—fell silent. The pride and excitement of the day was being stifled. "Graduation, the hush-hush magic time of frills and gifts and congratulations and diplomas, was finished for me before my name was called, we were nothing."[lix]

Then Henry Reed rose to give his valedictorian speech. Angelou questioned the point of it all when he began to quote Shakespeare's Hamlet. "'To Be or Not to Be.' Hadn't he heard the whitefolks? We couldn't be, so the question was a waste of time."[lx] I doubt she was the only child that felt this way. Over and over again Black children have been and are still being told that there are limits to their goals, limits to their aspirations, and limits to their imaginations—especially if they come from urban environments and/or from poor and working-class families. They were told that they could not truly and fully be. And as Angelou noted, aspirations for the Black girls especially are so often left out. So, one could conclude that pursuing any goals was a waste of time. But in the midst of this reminder of these limits, Henry Reed had other plans.

> Then there was a hush, which in an audience warns that something unplanned is happening. I looked up and saw Henry Reed, the conservative, the proper, the A student, turn his back to the audience and turn to us (the proud graduating class of 1940) and sing, nearly speaking,
>
> > 'Lift ev'ry voice and sing
> > Till earth and heaven ring
> > Ring with the harmonies of Liberty'[lxi]

The music started, and the parents joined in, the other classes began to sing, and the kindergarten teacher brought her class on stage to sing. Henry Reed helped usher back in the spirit of the day. "We were on top again. As always, again. We survived. The depths had been icy and dark, but now a bright sun spoke to our souls. I was no longer simply a member of the proud graduating class of 1940; I was a proud member of the wonderful, beautiful Negro race."[lxii]

Angelou and her class knew this song as the Black National Anthem. "Every child I knew had learned that song with his ABC's and along with 'Jesus Loves Me This I Know.'"[lxiii] What had been given to Angelou, her classmates, and her community were resources that would help them overcome the limits placed upon them by the wider society. In the existing societal structure, the oppressive class, as represented by this elected official, had set limits on their achievements and would do everything in their power to make sure that the existing system was left in place. Henry Reed imagined a different world, and he used the resources given him to remind his audience that they had long before been taught that they were, in fact, limitless. So, they enacted their historical imagination and remembered those that walked before them that had been knocked down and gotten up, and they knew that they too could get back up. They remembered the lesson of strength, and they sang.

When done well, education stimulates individuals to be better: better thinkers, better citizens, better innovators, better people. In turn, students will seek and demand better: a better life, a better society, a better world. The teaching ministry of the Church, therefore, ought to be rooted in this type of education—education that make us our better selves and builds community. A congregation that embraces the notion of ubuntu in its ecclesiastical identity is primed for engaging in Christian Education and spiritual formation of youth that make us better in this way.

Christian Education as Sharing Wisdom

At an urban majority African American congregation I served, children would be invited up during the worship service for what they called "Wisdom Keeping." During this time, children and adults would share knowledge. Often, an adult would pass down knowledge that included Bible stories, Christian traditions (especially during Advent, Lent, and Holy Days), and congregational history. The first Sunday of Advent, the children would learn and re-learn about the Advent wreath and the purpose of the Advent season. On the day the congregation celebrated their anniversary, the story was told to the children about how the congregation had formed. They were reminded that it had started as a youth outreach program and that the original youth group of the church had chosen the name that would eventually become the congregation's name. There were times that the children, in turn, were responsible for sharing their wisdom. Every February, for example, the children were tasked with presenting information on Black historical figures. They may have also been called upon to share the stories of faith through song or drama during this time.

I was unfamiliar with the term "wisdom keeping" and asked why we referred to this time in this manner. I was told that it was important to be clear about the intention, which was to share wisdom that needed to be kept within the community, not necessarily in a private secret kind of way, but because things that are not kept, are lost. There was an understanding that among the Black community, a special time of training and honing needed to happen within the walls of the church and that children needed to be trained to understand what it meant to be a Black Christian child growing up in this particular community. This was especially true in this urban environment where many of the young people lived. With so many unhealthy options trying to claim these youth, this congregation saw the importance of sharing and keeping the wisdom in this way to remind the youth who they are and whose they are.

This time of Wisdom Keeping is a small part of a larger understanding of the type of Christian Education emphasis needed to nurture the sanctified imagination. A mentoring congregation that is steeped in an understanding of emancipatory ecclesiology is primed to approach their Christian Education in a manner beyond simply passing down information or by indoctrinating young people and making sure that they have the "right" answers. To nurture the sanctified imagination, we charge young people and their congregations to form and keep wisdom.

The work of Anne Wimberly and Evelyn Parker as presented in their text *In Search of Wisdom: Faith Formation in the Black Church* present three basic tenants of wisdom formation that are extremely helpful in further understanding the difference between forming and keeping wisdom and merely passing on information. First, teachers who seek to nurture wisdom must be aware of the complexity of life. "We form wisdom as we come to honest awareness that there are some dilemmas in life for which no easy resolution will come."[lxiv] Forming wisdom is messy. The problems urban youth face are immense, and teachers lie to their students when they try to give simplistic answers to complicated problems. The lack of easy resolutions, however, does not negate the need to provide paradigms and resources for the ones seeking resolution.

Second, "Christian wisdom formation refers to our ongoing journey of imagining, gaining insights, and deciding how to live as faithful and responsible Christians."[lxv] Understanding the journey is especially important for youth because understanding their journey also means understanding their development mentally, faithfully, and psychologically. Respecting the journey also means respecting different starting points and paths. Yet together we move towards the common goal of being faithful and responsible Christians and supporting each other in all the different ways that goal manifests itself.

Thirdly, this concept recognizes the need for an entire congregation and community to be involved with the faith formation of children. It is intergenerational. The training of youth is not relegated to a few credentialed individuals; it is the role of the congregation as a whole to raise children in faith. This concept necessitates communal teaching and communal celebration. Wisdom formation and nurturing, then, is done in a congregation seeking to embody ubuntu. This type of sharing of wisdom is a concrete way congregations can participate in intergenerational Christian Education and continue to hone their collective sanctified imaginations.

Christian Education as Critical Pedagogy

Teaching for critical consciousness calls for a critical pedagogy.[7] Critical pedagogy refers to an educational practice grounded in a vision for justice and equality. Centering Christian Education in critical pedagogy makes this type of education not only a social and educational vision, but a theological one as well. As I argued in Chapter One, mainstream education is designed to benefit those within the center. Benefiting the center intrinsically means ignoring voices that challenge the status quo. These voices are ignored because the goal is to keep the center safe. Those on the margins often do not see themselves in the content of the materials covered, nor are their familiar ways of learning often presented as useful knowledge or wisdom worth keeping. A critical pedagogy, however, aims to amplify the

---

[7] Definitions for critical pedagogy are as diverse and dynamic as those who practice it. For my work, I draw mostly on the work of Paulo Freire and bell hooks with a little help in framing from Joe Kincheloe.

voices and the concerns of those who speak from the margins. Critical pedagogy also teaches the importance of resisting the influence of the dominant power and is dedicated to the alleviation of human suffering. These factors make critical pedagogy an important foundation for Christian Education seeking to nurture the sanctified imagination. Educating for a critical consciousness addresses two of the issues I have noted as blocking the imagination: low sense of self-worth and an educational system that re-creates the status quo. As a broken education system leads to a low sense of self-worth, critical pedagogy is needed to raise one's sense of self-worth and role in contributing to community formation.

"Critical pedagogy is interested in maintaining a delicate balance between social change and cultivating the intellect—developing a rigorous education in a hostile environment that accomplishes both goals."[lxvi] It is no coincidence that freedom movements often start as student movements. Youth possess the passion that drives change. Yet, working for social change demands an understanding of current events and philosophies, a historical understanding of how these philosophies came to be dominant, a knowledge of differing theories and philosophies, and the intellectual ability to create a different dominant thought. I highlight these characteristics because mainstream education does not encourage students to challenge the status quo, to think critically about what they are learning, or to imagine different interpretations. Therefore, ministering to youth who are not served well from mainstream education—like those that may come from struggling urban schools—requires an alternative form of education. Christian Education rooted in critical pedagogy is needed in congregations in order to nurture the sanctified imagination. This may sound off-putting to some who argue that the role of Christian Education with youth lies in giving them a set of information that includes truths they should not question. They may further argue that one ought not think critically about the Bible or Church tradition, but instead should learn and submit to its teachings. These same practitioners fail to see how teaching their particular reading of the text and not empowering youth to claim their own readings, their own voices, and their own word from God, also does not empower youth to claim their own connection to God and God's work. This kind of teaching does not empower; it colonizes. Decolonizing Christian Education frees youth to see how God is working in the world and imagine how God can continue to work in the world through and with them—this is theological imagination that is liberating. With this theological imagination nurtured, youth are not bound to what they see around them or what they have been told they can be. They are free to break from these narratives and create a different story for themselves. This is the type of wisdom I seek to form.

The concepts of critical consciousness, as we understand it today, come primarily from the work of Paulo Freire. After living among impoverished peasants and learning about poverty and oppression, Freire began his work as an educator in order to improve the lives of marginalized and oppressed people. He referred to this work as liberatory action. As he sought a way to engage with learners that was different from the mainstream education that had aided in their oppression, his liberatory action is rooted in an understanding of *conscientização*—conscientization or critical consciousness. Indeed, for Freire this required more than an inward change, it required outward action. Freire spoke against what he referred to as the banking concept of education. This concept assumes that the student knows nothing and comes to the teacher to passively receive information. The students should then be ready to give this information back at the given time. In this model, the students are the objects while the teacher is the subject of learning – a completely teacher-driven academic style. Freire imagined a different way. Recognizing the passivity of education, Freire introduced "cultural circles."

> Instead of a teacher, we had a coordinator; instead of lectures, dialogue; instead of pupils, group participants; instead of alienation syllabi, compact programs that were "broken down" and "codified" into learning units.[lxvii]

Freire was able to read his context and create a program for those within his care. While Freire's praxis is not transferrable to every context, the foundational theories are helpful to all seeking to work with those in the margins and for the purpose of this work, consider his understandings of critical consciousness, dialogue, and the role of the teacher and how they help nurture the youth with whom we work.

In short, critical consciousness is a way of looking at and being aware of one's community and the world at large in a way that understands and challenges the way society runs. Teaching for critical consciousness while nurturing a young person's imagination grounds the action in reality and distinguishes imagination from fantasy or wishful thinking. Critical consciousness requires reflection and action, but first it requires that we teach not only through lecture (where only one person has a voice), but that we teach also through dialogue. The teacher is not assumed to be the one with all-knowing wisdom pouring the information into the brain of the passive student. Dialogue presupposes a conversation amongst partners with equal voice.

"Founding itself upon love, humility, and faith, dialogue becomes a horizontal relationship of which mutual trust between the dialoguers is the logical consequence."[lxviii] Dialogue as a teaching method works well within a bidirectional mentoring relationship. No longer a top-down relationship, the teacher and student enter a horizontal relationship. This horizontal relationship was imperative for Freire's work with adults, but as with bidirectional mentoring, it gets a little complicated when working with youth because of their unequal authority. However, unequal authority does not mean an inequality in voice or value. The goal then is to first find an alternative that lies between a top-down and horizontal relationship. Like the relationship between dialoguers, it must be rooted first in love. Congregations must first look for adults that love the youth—not pity them, nor feel sorry for them, nor want to fix them, but first and foremost, have a profound love for them and the Image of God within them. These adults must embrace humility. This type of teaching is messy. It begins by noting that the teacher does not have all of the answers. This is a soul-baring process—one that must be entered humbly, and with faith and hope. The underlying premise is the belief that there can be change. In light of all the difficulties along the way the adult cannot lose hope. As Freire argues, "Hope is rooted in men's incompletion, from which they move out in constant search—a search which can be carried out only in communion with others."[lxix] The search for hope also needs to be carried out in communion with God. Freire goes on to characterize hopelessness as a form of silencing. In order to add voice, one needs the Divine as well as others. And if adults working with youth are to combat personal hopelessness, they themselves can never lose hope.

Educating for critical consciousness also means that we must look at teaching technique and the role of the teacher. The revolutionary teacher must also be ready to be transformed. "The revolutionary's role is to liberate, and be liberated, with the people—not to win them over."[lxx] Freire also warns against programming with the teacher's purposes in mind. We are not to run programs that have nothing to do with learners' desires and dreams. The purpose is not to give learners something we think they should have, but to dialogue with them about our joint worldviews and inform each other. If we hold our worldviews to be always right, then we are simply trying to impart something our students should ingest and not challenge. We are, therefore, participating in the problematic banking concept of education. We ought not to come up with a program that is simply presented to the learners. All education must be done in conjunction with teacher and pupil—with a recognition that these roles are not static, but fluid as the teacher also learns from the pupil. "We must realize that their view of the world, manifested variously in their action, reflects their *situation* in the world."[lxxi] Conscientization is not meant to be an end unto itself, it has to be constantly practiced. The goal is to find contextualized ways to continually educate for critical consciousness.

Forming One's Voice and One's Story

There are several ways that critical pedagogy can facilitate the nurturing of young people's sanctified imaginations. A current Christian Education method fitting this type of conscientization is story theology. As a method of Christian Education, story theology finds meaning in everyday stories and asks what we can learn about God and our role as those who work for God. Just as the stories of the Bible reveal God's nature as God operated among humans, we ask, how do our stories and the stories of those around us inform us about God's movements and guidance? As we all share our stories and find meaning in each other's stories, story theology also reimagines the role of the leader. It is based on dialogue and giving voice, must be done in communion with others and God, and ends with movement into liberatory action. Story theology is also used within Christian Education to remind people that they are a part of God's continuing story. Two such paradigms can be found in Dori Baker's *Girlfriend Theology* and Anne Wimberly's *Soul Stories*. I refer to these models because both seek to liberate and empower groups that have been marginalized. Baker concentrates on adolescent girls while Wimberly focuses on African Americans. I will first describe key components of each model while noting the relevance of each component for working with marginalized populations. I will then compare these methods and show how, together, they help raise a person's sense of self-worth and hope and aid in nurturing a liberative theological imagination.

Dori Baker's *Doing Girlfriend Theology* is a story theology method created with and for adolescent girls. While Baker's work focuses on girls, she notes that the method can be used with different genders and in mixed gendered groups. With Baker's focus on girls and my focus on Black urban youth, we both center on youth that have been marginalized; thus, much of Baker's work can be used with urban youth as we have similar goals. We both seek a method of Christian Education that those that have been marginalized can use to create a world that fosters human flourishing. We also recognize that if those marginalized young people listen to and internalize the voices that seek to limit them, they are not living their full lives, the lives that God created them to live. We both recognize the need for marginalized youth to view their lives theologically, to take steps toward transformation and vocation, and to constantly seek to see how God is calling them to move within a particular situation. Girlfriend theology combats the forces seeking to internalize the voices of girls by creating a pedagogical model that begins with the girls' life stories. "It engages those stories with the stories of adult women who have found voice and translates the resources of women's theological thought into the context of female adolescence."[lxxii] The equal sharing between girls and adult women that have found voice make this a relational model and is a useful paradigm for a bi-directional mentoring relationship.

Girlfriend Theology has four movements: hearing the story; experiencing the near; experiencing the distant; and going forth. In the first movement, an individual girl shares her story while others are asked to listen. While listeners may have the story in front of them, they are asked not to read along and only to refer to the written story if needed for clarification. In the second movement, girls may ask for points of clarification, without getting caught up in what happens next in the narrative. Girls are also invited to share thoughts and emotions that the story conjured up for them. In the third movement, girls are asked to raise and think about some larger themes and theological issues that are present within the shared story. They are also asked to express where they see God at work within the story. In the final movement, girls consider how the hearing of this story has changed them and what God may be saying to them as a group and as individuals.

The girlfriend theology paradigm works well coupled with Ann Wimberly's story-linking paradigm. Wimberly's *Soul Stories* presents a story theology practiced within several African American Christian faith traditions and affirms story-linking as a story theology paradigm. Story-linking occurs when different types of stories are linked together to find commonalities and assist participants in understanding what it is God is calling them to do. Three primary stories are integral parts of the story-linking process: (1) the stories of our everyday lives, (2) the story of God and the good news of Jesus Christ in Scripture, and (3) post-biblical Christian faith heritage stories, particularly those from the African American Christian faith heritage.[lxxiii] The first three phases of the process engage the sharing and linking of these stories. There is also a fourth phase, which in many ways is the culminating phase. The fourth phase involves Christian ethical decision-making. "Participants become involved in two activities in phase four. In these activities, they discern God's call for concrete liberating and vocational action, and they decide concrete actions."[lxxiv] The goal is to provide practical tools that enable the participants to make faithful life choices.

Phase One engages the everyday story. "We either consciously or unconsciously use our own personal stories as a lens through which we view what is being focused on in Christian Education."[lxxv] Identifying this as a natural tendency and an empowering activity, Wimberly, like Baker, encourages beginning with our personal stories. Wimberly presents six components that contribute to our stories that affect our liberation and vocation: identity, social contexts, interpersonal relationships, life events, life meanings, and our unfolding story plot. Presenting the telling of our personal story in this way can be very helpful to urban youth. So often, they see their stories as isolated from everything around them. Realizing that these six components, along with others, intertwine to create their story may make them feel less isolated as they share a few of these components with others. Also, starting with one's own story recognizes the validity and importance of everyone's story, for everyone has an important story to tell.

The second phase is engaging the faith story in the Bible. The personal story is linked with a story in Scripture through an overarching theme. With so many stories to choose from within the Biblical text, one can be found that have similarities to one's personal story. The linking of a Biblical story reminds us how our stories are not separate from God's grand narrative. Instead our stories are a part of God's story. Story-linking helps us to realize that many aspects of our story have been lived before and God has dealt with it in various ways—it is an act of historical imagination. If God was able to move then, that same God can move now—even if the movement is not identical. This phase allows us to see ourselves as part of God's people, and to see our stories as attesting to the God's continuing movement among God's people. When working with youth, it is essential to center the stories of youth within the Biblical text. Stories of God moving upon a young David, choosing to be incarnated through a young Mary, or creating reform through a young king Josiah can empower youth to recognize that God can also work as powerfully through them.

Phase Three of the story-linking process is designed to link components of the everyday life story and the story from the Bible with shared heritage stories from Black Christian faith traditions. The goal is to focus on a story of shared history. The stories of Africans in the Americas are stories of struggle and triumph. We can see God delivering people from very desperate situations and God's people making some very difficult decisions. For work with urban youth, I would also use stories from current events and pop culture in addition to historical stories.

Phase Four incorporates discerning God's call for concrete action and deciding upon which concrete actions to take. Wimberly and Parker state,

> If Christian Education activities are to result in liberating wisdom that moves persons toward liberation and hope-building vocation, they must give attention to meanings of a commitment to faithful and responsible Christian action. These activities assume that we as African Americans have a continuing stake in the liberation and vocational direction of others.[lxxvi]

The story-linking process allows us to link our stories with other stories in order to see how God has moved in the past. The thought is, if God has moved in the past, then God can move in the present. Once the stories have been linked and analyzed, the question becomes: How is God calling us to move now? This is the question at the heart of a theological imagination. What needs to be created now? How is God leading us to create it? By recounting biblical stories and stories from a shared heritage, we can move forward in confidence with a God that has proven time and time again to be a powerful force that moves within and among people and allows ordinary people to do extraordinary things.

Both story theology paradigms can be used to empower those that have been marginalized. They both assume and assert that we all have stories to tell. They help urban youth to claim their voice. Not only are these stories worthy of being told, they must be told as a continuation of God's story. The telling of an individual's story is used as a resource of catechesis that then engages, encourages, and enlightens others. The mere fact that a group *is* marginalized means that they have been told that their lives and stories are not as important as others. They have been taught by society that at best, their lived lives are *literally* marginal to the main story. Story theology combats this false teaching and empowers people by valuing and honoring their lives and what God has done for them. Both paradigms start with liberation and end with a call for action—they are paradigms that help facilitate the development of a critical consciousness. The goal is not only to be affirmed but also to leave changed and empowered to make changes in our personal life and in the lives and communities of those around us. Through the telling of their stories, and hearing of others, people are empowered to make a difference. That difference, of course, needs to be rooted in God and a vision that one creates with God using the sanctified theological imagination.

When Nia's youth minister puts these theories and paradigms in conversation with each other, it aids Nia several ways. She needs education for critical consciousness to combat the miseducation that she most likely received. Nia's formal education has trained her to go along with the status quo. However, for Nia, the status quo is problematic and does not serve her well. Developing critical consciousness will help Nia to see what is problematic in her environment; she will be able to see it through a new lens. Educating for critical consciousness within a congregation's walls creates the fertile ground for this new lens to be a theological one. Nia can begin to see herself a little through God's eyes. Learning to challenge the misinformation fed to her by society helps improve her sense of self-worth while combatting personal hopelessness.

These theories and paradigms further the nurturing of a sanctified theological imagination. A sanctified theological imagination involves seeing one's self through God's eyes. A critical consciousness is a tool needed to be able to create a different future in one's mind. Story theology also gives Nia an avenue for seeing with a Godly lens; it nurtures the sanctified imagination by casting her story as part of God's larger story. She learns that her story is important and worthy of sharing. She also learns a communal and historical story. Through bidirectional mentoring, she can not only share her story, but hear her mentor's story and the story of different generations and learn the power of their collective voices. Through this sharing and hearing, she develops initiative and solidarity.

In Angelou's text, aspects of the sanctified imagination are also on display. Henry Reed shows the power of Sankofa. Like that mystical bird, the young adolescent moves forward equipped with an understanding of past resiliency. With this past resiliency and historical imagination ever present, Henry Reed carries the fragile egg that is the potential of community before him and says that, no matter what others say, we will walk forward. The naysayers cannot make a path for us—in fact, they have, but we are not interested in that narrowly prescribed path. We will make our own path. May we help Nia to move in this same direction.

Epilogue

Sending Forth: Nurturing Nia's Sanctified Imagination

There is a common conversation I have with the seminarians I teach when they have just read a book that they like and think would be helpful to their ministry. It begins with them expressing their gratitude for the text and then saying something like, "I can't wait to do this at my church." They then name a particular problem they have and how the book gives them a way to solve it. My response is always the same: Take a beat. I understand the desire to read something one day and implement it the next day; I was that seminarian and minister. I saw a need I didn't know how to fill or a problem I couldn't solve, and then this magical text (or workshop or lecture) would seemingly fall into my lap and, even before I had digested the closing sentence, I was off to the races and ready to implement. Then, inevitably, I became the disappointed minister who implemented this new (for me) way of looking at ministry and then got frustrated by the fact that it wasn't easy, it didn't always work because I did not take my context into account, and it did not solve all my problems. There are no magic pills. So, take a beat. Be grateful that you read something that moves you. Sit with it. Take time to read your context and see what can be gleaned from the text for your context and remember that there is no magic pill.

A helpful response to Nia and the many youth like her lies not in magic, but in hope. My desire is to help replace the personal hopelessness I have seen in so many of the teens I have served, with hope and the realization that they are not stuck with a predetermined path, but that they can create their own with God, the people of God that God has placed around then, and their God-given imagination. My prayer is that, with these God-given eyes, they will see new ways of being in the world as the community around them embraces this as well. I know that this is the prayer of many youth ministers, a prayer I hope that this text can help answer. So, let us take a collective beat and sit with this for a minute.

As we collectively sit and reflect, I want to quickly pull together the different pieces of the texts to once again see how they work together to empower urban youth. My basic premise is that by nurturing the sanctified imagination, young people can get the new vision Delores Williams speaks about when discussing Hagar. The goal is to give young people theological resources in addition to regular life skills. Life skills allow one to make decisions based on what is presented. The lens of one's sanctified imagination allows one to see things that are beyond what may be in front of you, not in a way that promotes magical or wishful thinking, but in a way that promotes hope.

Imagination feeds on imagination. So, the entire ecclesiastical identity of the congregation that nurtures these young people matters in profound ways. The congregation ought to be a place that realizes the importance of every believer, regardless of age. As congregations imagine together, it is beneficial for youth to have a mentor. In a congregation that embraces the ecclesiastical promise that ubuntu presents, bidirectional mentoring is a more organic experience. Yet, bi-directional mentoring can happen in many different situations. There are a variety of contextual ways to provide fertile ground for space for youth and adults to imagine and work together. We listen to young people's voices and build with them. We also teach critical thinking, and through these bi-directional mentoring relationships, we encourage youth to challenge us as we challenge them to always question what they are being presented. We use these skills to open up the entire community to imagine together and see things in different ways. All of this is in the hopes of empowering young people like Nia.

Nia is a gestalt because there are many young people with her story or stories similar to hers. And for whatever reason, they come from a place of personal hopelessness, but my prayer is that we remind them that hope exists. My prayer is not only for the Nias of the world, but also for all of the youth ministers that care for their own Nias and find it hard to nurture their own sanctified imagination. Nurturing others' imaginations will nurture one's own imagination as well. Things do not have to continue being the way that they are. There are different ways; and together, youth, those that love youth, and those called to nurture these youth, with the help of God's Spirit, can imagine those ways together.

Endnotes

i. Mitchem, S.Y. (2002). *Introducing Womanist Theology*. New York: Orbis Books, p. 77.

ii. Ibid.

iii. Chang, H. (2008). *Autoethnography as Method*, Developing Qualitative Inquiry. Walnut Creek, California: Left Coast Press, Inc., p. 48.

iv. Ibid., 49.

v. Hofer, J. (1934). Medical Dissertation on Nostalgia. *Bulletin of the History of Medicine, 2*: 376-391.

vi. Boym, S. (2001). *The Future of Nostalgia*. New York: Basic Books, p. xiii.

vii. Goulding, C. (1999). Heritage, Nostalgia, and 'Grey' Consumer. *Journal of Marketing Practice: Applied Marketing Science, 5*(6).

viii. Gammon, S. (2002). Fantasy, Nostalgia and the Pursuit of What Never Was. In *Sport Tourism: Principle and Practice*. Eds. Gammon, S. & Kurtzman, J. Eastbourne, UK: Leisure Studies Association, 61-72.

ix. Boym, S. (2001). *The Future of Nostalgia*. New York: Basic Books, p. 10.

x. Ibid, xv.

xi. Brunious, L. (1996). *How Black Disadvantaged Adolescents Socially Construct Reality: Listen, Do You Hear What I Hear?* New York: The Continuum Publishing Company, p. 105–106.

xii. Ibid.

xiii. The Editorial Projects in Education Research Center. (2011). Diplomas Count 2011: Beyond High School, Before Baccalaureate. *Education Week, 30*(34).

xiv. Education Trust. (2013, Jul. 30). Closing the Gap Data Points. *Education Trust*, last modified October 15, 2009, Retrieved from www.Edtrust.org/dc/publication/closing-the-gaps-data-points.

xv. Fulgham, N. (2013). *Educating All God's Children: What Christians Can--and Should--Do to Improve Public Education for Low-Income Kids*. Grand Rapids, Michigan: Brazos Press, p. 15–16.

xvi. Brunious, L. (1996). *How Black Disadvantaged Adolescents Socially Construct Reality: Listen, Do You Hear What I Hear?* New York: The Continuum Company, p. 33.

xvii. Ibid., 13.

xviii. Ibid., 141.

xix. Ibid., 192.

xx. bell hooks. (2003). *Rock My Soul: Black People and Self Esteem*. New York: Washington Square Press, p. 19.

xxi. Ibid., 193.

xxii. hooks, *Teaching Critical Thinking: Practical Wisdom*, 60.

xxiii. Ibid., 61.

xxiv. Ibid., 60.

xxv. Wesley, J. (1991). The Scripture Way of Salvation. In *John Wesley's Sermons: An Anthology*. Eds., Albert C. Outler and Richard Heitzenrater. Nashville: Abingdon, p. 488.

xxvi. Wesley, J. (1991). The Marks of New Birth. In *John Wesley's Sermons: An Anthology*. Eds., Albert C. Outler and Richard Heitzenrater. Nashville: Abingdon.

xxvii. Wesley, J. (1994). *The Works of John Wesley Volume XIV*. Ed. Thomas Jackson. Franklin, TN: Providence House, p. 321.

xxviii. Wesley, J. (1991). The Scripture Way of Salvation. In *John Wesley's Sermons: An Anthology*. Eds., Albert C. Outler and Richard Heitzenrater. Nashville: Abingdon.

xxix. Kwok, P. (1989) Discovering the Bible in the Non-Biblical World. In *Semeia* 47:25-42,125.

xxx.   Kwok, P. (2005). *Postcolonial Imagination and Feminist Theology*. Louisville: Westminster John Knox Press, p. 125.

xxxi.   Ibid., 38.

xxxii.   *Ibid.*, 49.

xxxiii.   Migliorie, D. (2004). *Faith Seeking Understanding: An Introduction to Christian Theology*, 2nd ed. Grand Rapids, Michigan: William B. Eerdmans Publishing Company, p. 256–257.

xxxiv.   Parker, E.L. (2003). *Trouble Don't Last Always: Emancipatory Hope Among African American Adolescents*. Cleveland: The Pilgrim Press, p. 11.

xxxv.   Braxton, B.R. (2002). *No Longer Slaves: Galatians and African American Experience*. Collegeville, MN: Michael Glazier/Liturgical Press, p. 93.

xxxvi.   Ibid., 94.

xxxvii.   Ibid.

xxxviii.   Ibid., 70.

xxxix.   Miguez, N.O. (2004). Galatians. In *Global Bible Commentary*. Nashville: Abingdon Press, p. 468.

xl.   Ibid.

xli.   Ibid.

xlii.   Ibid.

xliii.   Lienenmann-Perrin, C. (2004). The Biblical Foundations for a Feminist and Participatory Theology of Mission. *International Review of Mission, 93*, p. 23.

xliv.   Battle, M. (2009). *Ubuntu: I in You and You in Me*. New York, New York: Seabury Books, p. 2.

xlv.   "I Need You to Survive," (2002). Album, track 12 on Hezekiah Walker and the Love Fellowship Crusade Choir, *Family Affair II – Live At Radio City Music Hall,* Verity Records.

xlvi.   Fine, M. & Weis, L. (1998). *The Unknown City: Lives of Poor and Working Class Young Adults*. Boston: Beacon Press, 1998.

xlvii.   Deutsch, N. (2008). *Pride in the Projects: Teens Building Identities in Urban Contexts*. New York and London: New York University Press, p. 9.

xlviii. Parks, S. (2000). *Big Questions, Worthy Dreams: Mentoring Young Adults in Their Search for Meaning, Purpose, and Faith*. San Francisco: Jossey-Bass, p. 6.

xlix.   Ibid., 23.

l.   Ibid., 93.

li.   Carter, T. (2004, Apr.) Recipe for Growth: Executives Learn From Employees Lower Down on the Food Chain. *American Bar Association Journal, 90*(4): 85.

lii.   Creps, E. (2008). *Reverse Mentoring: How Young Leaders Can Transform the Church and Why We Should Let Them*. Leadership Network. San Francisco: Josey-Bass, p. xviii.

liii.   Fowler, J.W. (2000). *Becoming Adult, Becoming Christian: Adult Development and Christian Faith*. San Francisco: Jossey-Bass, p. 47.

liv.   Fowler, J.W. (1981). *Stages of Faith: The Psychology of Human Development and the Quest for Meaning*. San Francisco: HarperSan Francisco, A Division of HarperCollins Publishers, p. 173.

lv.   Ibid.

lvi.   Ibid., 75.

lvii.   Ibid., 77.

lviii.   Angelou, M. (1969). *I Know Why the Caged Bird Sings*. New York: Bantam Books, p. 179.

lix.   Ibid., 180.

lx.   Ibid., 175.

lxi.   Ibid., 182.

lxii.   Ibid., 183.

lxiii.   Ibid., 184.

lxiv.   Ibid., 183.

lxv.   Wimberly, A.E.S. & Parker, E.L. (2002). *In Search of Wisdom: Faith Formation in the Black Church*. Nashville: Abingdon Press, p. 13.

lxvi.   Ibid., 12–13.

lxvii.   Kincheloe, J. (2008). *Critical Pedagogy Primer 2nd Edition*. New York: Peter Lang Publishing, p. 21.

lxviii. Freire, P. (2008). *Education for Critical Consciousness*. London/New York: The Continuum Publishing Company, p. 38.

lxix.   Freire, P. (2008). *Pedagogy of the Oppressed*. London/New York: The Continuum Publishing Company, p. 91.

lxx.   Ibid.

lxxi.   Ibid., 95.

lxxii.   Ibid., 96.

lxxiii. Baker, D.G. (2005). *Doing Girlfriend Theology: God Talk with Yong Women*. Cleveland: The Pilgrim Press, p. 17.

lxxiv.   Wimberly, A.E.S. (2005). *Soul Stories: African American Christian Education*, Revised. Nashville: Abingdon Press, p. 25.

lxxv.   Ibid., 33.

lxxvi.   Ibid., 26.

lxxvii. Ibid., 33.

Bibliography

African American Policy Forum. (2008). A Primer on Intersectionality. *African American Policy Forum*. Retrieved from http://static.squarespace.com/static/53f20d90e4b0b80451158d8c/53f 399a5e4b029c2ffbe26cc/53f399c8e4b029c2ffbe2b28/1408473544947/ 59819079-Intersectionality-Primer.pdf?format=original

Allen, H.C., & Ross, C.L. (2012). *Intergenerational Christian Formation: Bringing the Whole Church Together in Ministry, Community and Worship*. Downers Grove, IL: InterVarsity Press.

Angelou, M. (1969). *I Know Why the Caged Bird Sings*. New York: Bantam Books.

Baker, D.G. (2005). *Doing Girlfriend Theology: God Talk with Yong Women*. Cleveland: The Pilgrim Press.

Baker, D.G., & Mercer, J.A. (2007). *Lives to Offer: Accompanying Youth on Their Vocational Quests*. Youth Ministry Alternatives. Cleveland, OH: The Pilgrim Press.

Battle, M. (2009). *Ubuntu: I in You and You in Me*. New York: Seabury Books.

Bettie, J. (2003). *Women Without Class: Girls, Race, and Identity*. Berkley: University of California Press.

Boym, S. (2001). *The Future of Nostalgia*. New York: Basic Books.

Braxton, B.R. (2002). *No Longer Slaves: Galatians and African American Experience*. Collegeville, MN: Michael Glazier/Liturgical Press.

Brown, L.M., & Gilligan, C. (1992). *Meeting at the Crossroads: Women's Psychology and Girl's Development*. New York: Ballantine Books.

Browning, D.S. (1991). *A Fundamental Practical Theology: Descriptive and Strategic Proposals*. Minneapolis, MN: Fortress Press.

Brueggemann, W. (2001). *The Prophetic Imagination*. Minneapolis, MN: Fortress Press.

Brueggemann, W. (2012). *The Practice of Prophetic Imagination: Preaching an Emancipatory Word*. Minneapolis, MN: Fortress Press.

Brunious, L. (1996). *How Black Disadvantaged Adolescents Socially Construct Reality: Listen, Do You Hear What I Hear?* New York: The Continuum Publishing Company.

Cannon, K.G. (1996). *Katie's Canon: Womanism and the Soul of the Black Community*. New York: The Continuum Publishing Company.

Carroll, R. (1997). *Sugar in the Raw: Voices of Young Black Girls in America*. New York: Three Rivers Press.

Carter, S.M, & Little, M. (2007). Justifying Knowledge, Justifying Method, Taking Action: Epistemologies, Methodologies, and Methods in Qualitative Research. *Qualitative Health Research, 17*(1316).

Carter, T. (2004, April). Recipe for Growth: Executives Learn From Employees Lower Down on the Food Chain. *American Bar Association Journal, 90*(4), 85.

Chang, H. (2008). *Autoethnography as Method*. Developing Qualitative Inquiry. Walnut Creek, California: Left Coast Press, Inc.

Clark, C., & Powell, K. (2007). *Deep Justice in a Broken World: Helping Your Kids Serve Others and Right the Wrongs Around Them*. Grand Rapids, MI: Zondervan.

Collins, P.H. (1998). It's All in the Family: Intersections of Gender, Race, and Nation. In *Border Crossings: Multicultural and Postcolonial Feminist Challenges to Philosophy (Part 2). Hypatia, 13*, 62–82. Indiana: Indiana University Press.

Collins, P.H. (2000). *Black Feminist Thought: Knowledge, Consciousness, and the Politics of Empowerment*. New York: Routledge.

Coontz, S. (1992). *The Way We Never Were: American Families and the Nostalgia Trap*. New York: Basic Books.

Copeland, M.S. (2006). A Thinking Margin: The Womanist Movement as Critical Cognitive Praxis. In *Deeper Shades of Purple: Womanism in Religion and Society*, edited by Stacey Floyd-Thomas, 226–235. New York and London: New York University Press.

Corbman, M. (2005). *A Tiny Step Away From Deepest Faith: A Teenager's Search for Meaning*. Brewster, MA: Paraclete Press.

Crenshaw, K. (1995). Mapping the Margins: Intersectionality, Identity Politics, and Violence Against Women of Color. In *Critical Race Theory: The Key Writings That Formed a Movement*. New York: The New Press.

Creps, E. (2008). *Reverse Mentoring: How Young Leaders Can Transform the Church and Why We Should Let Them*. Leadership Network. San Francisco: Josey-Bass.

Davis, F. (1979). *Yearning for Yesterday: A Sociology of Nostalgia*. New York - London: The Free Press, A Division of Macmillan Publishing Co., Inc.

Delgado, R. (1995). *Critical Race Theory: The Cutting Edge*. Philadelphia: Temple University Press.

Deutsch, N. (2008). *Pride in the Projects: Teens Building Identities in Urban Contexts*. New York and London: New York University Press.

Dunn, J.D.G. (1993). *The Theology of Paul's Letter to the Galatians*. Cambridge: Cambridge University Press.

Ebo, R.N. (1996). "Lord, Why Did You Make Me Black?" In *God Has All You Need: Because All You Need Is God?* Self-published through Lulu Distribution Services.

Education Trust. (2009, Oct. 15). Closing the Gap Data Points. *Education Trust* Retrieved from www.Edtrust.org/dc/publication/closing-the-gaps-data-points

Ellis, C., Adams, T.E., & Bochner, A.P. (2001, Jan.) Autoethnography: An Overview. *Forum: Qualitative Social Research, 12*(1).

Erikson, E. (1968). *Identity: Youth and Crisis*. New York - London: W. W. Norton & Company, Inc.

Feinstein, S.G. (2009). *Secrets of the Teenage Brain: Research-Based Strategies for Reaching and Teaching Today's Adolescents*. Thousand Oaks, CA: Corwin, A SAGE Company.

Fine, M., & Weis, L. (1998). *The Unknown City: The Lives of Poor and Working Class Young Adults*. Boston: Beacon Press.

Floyd-Thomas, S. (2006). Introduction: Writing for Our Lives--Womanism as an Epistemological Revolution. In *Deeper Shades of Purple: Womanism in Religion and Society*, edited by Stacey Floyd-Thomas, 1–16. New York and London: New York University Press.

Fowler, J.W. (1981). *Stages of Faith: The Psychology of Human Development and the Quest for Meaning*. San Francisco: HarperSan Francisco, A Division of HarperCollins Publishers.

Fowler, J.W. (2000). *Becoming Adult, Becoming Christian: Adult Development and Christian Faith*. San Francisco: Jossey-Bass.

Freire, P. (1998) *Pedagogy of Freedom: Ethics, Democracy, and Civic Courage*. Translated by Patrick Clarke. Lanham - Boulder - New York - Oxford: Rowman & Littlefield Publishers, Inc.

Freire, P. (2008). *Education for Critical Consciousness*. London/New York: The Continuum Publishing Company.

Freire, P. (2009). *Pedagogy of the Oppressed*. Translated by Myra Bergman Ramos. 30th Anniversary. New York: The Continuum International Publishing Group.

Fulgham, N.B. (2013). *Educating All God's Children: What Christians Can-- and Should--Do to Improve Public Education for Low-Income Kids*. Grand Rapids, Michigan: Brazos Press.

Gammon, S. (2002). Fantasy, Nostalgia and the Pursuit That Never Was. In *Sport Tourism: Principle and Practice*, edited by Sean Gammon and Kurtzman, Joseph, 61–72. Eastbourne, UK: Leisure Studies Association.

Giroux, H. (2009). *Youth in a Suspect Society: Democracy or Disposability?* New York: Palgrave Macmillan.

Goulding, C. (1999). Heritage, Nostalgia, and 'Grey' Consumer. *Journal of Marketing Practice: Applied Marketing Science,* 5(6/7/8): 177–99. https://doi.org/10.1108/EUM0000000004573

Harris, M. (1987). *Teaching and Religious Imagination.* San Francisco: Harper & Row Publishers.

Harris, M., & Moran, G. (1997). Educating Persons. In *Mapping Christian Education: Approaches to Congregational Learning:* 58–73. Nashville: Abingdon Press.

Hille, K.H. (2007). *Religious Education in the African American Tradition: A Comprehensive Introduction.* St. Louis, MO: Chalice Press.

Hofer, J. (1934). Medical Dissertation on Nostalgia. Translated by Carolyn K. Anspach. *Bulletin of the History of Medicine,* 2: 376–91.

hooks, b. (1994). *Teaching to Transgress: Education as the Practice of Freedom.* New York: Routledge.

hooks, b. (2003). *Rock My Soul: Black People and Self Esteem.* New York: Washington Square Press.

hooks, b. (2010). *Teaching Critical Thinking: Practical Wisdom.* New York: Routledge.

Jennings, W.J. (2010). *The Christian Imagination: Theology and the Origins of Race.* New Haven/London: Yale University Press.

Kahl, B. (2000). No Longer Male: Masculinity Struggles Behind Galatians 3:28. *Journal for the Study of the New Testament,* 79.

Kincheloe, J. (2008). *Critical Pedagogy Primer.* New York: Peter Lang Publishing.

Kwok, P. (1989). Discovering the Bible in the Non-Biblical World. *Semeia,* 47: 25–42.

Kwok, P. (2005). *Postcolonial Imagination and Feminist Theology.* Louisville: Westminster John Knox Press.

Lienenmann-Perrin, C. (2004). The Biblical Foundations for a Feminist and Participatory Theology of Mission. *International Review of Mission,* 93.

Lockhart-Gilroy, A. (2016, Sep.). A Way Forward: Nurturing the Imagination at the Intersection of Race, Class, Gender, and Age. *Religious Education, 111*(4): 415–29.

Luther, M. (1979). *Commentary on Galatians*. Translated by Erasmus Middleton. Kregel Reprint Library Series. Grand Rapids, Michigan: Kregel Reprint Library Series.

McIntyre, J. (1987). *Faith Theology and Imagination*. Edinburgh: The Handsel Press Ltd.

Migliorie, D. (2004). *Faith Seeking Understanding: An Introduction to Christian Theology*. 2nd ed. Grand Rapids, Michigan: William B. Eerdmans Publishing Company.

Miguez, N.O. (2004). Galatians. In *Global Bible Commentary*. Nashville: Abingdon Press.

Mitchem, S.Y. (2002). *Introducing Womanist Theology*. New York: Orbis Books.

Parker, E.L. (2006). Nurturing the Sacred Self of Adolescent Girls. In *The Sacred Selves of Adolescent Girls*, edited by Evelyn L Parker. Cleveland: The Pilgrim Press.

Parker, E.L. (2003). *Trouble Don't Last Always: Emancipatory Hope Among African American Adolescents*. Cleveland: The Pilgrim Press.

Parks, S. (2000). *Big Questions, Worthy Dreams: Mentoring Young Adults in Their Search for Meaning, Purpose, and Faith*. San Francisco: Jossey-Bass.

Poling, J.N., & Miller, D.E. (1984, Spring) Foundations for a Practical Theology of Ministry. *Theological Education, 20*(2): 14–41.

Schipani, D. (1997). Education for Social Transformation. In *Mapping Christian Education: Approaches to Congregational Learning*, 23–40. Nashville: Abingdon Press.

Seymour, J., ed. (1997). *Mapping Christian Education: Approaches to Congregational Learning*. Nashville: Abingdon Press.

The Editorial Projects in Education Research Center. (2011). Diplomas Count 2011: Beyond High School, Before Baccalaureate, *Education Week, 30*(34).

Walker, H. & The Love Fellowship Crusade Choir. (2002). *I Need You to Survive*. Album. Track 12. Family Affair II: Live at Radio City Music Hall. Verity Records.

Wesley, J. (1991). *John Wesley's Sermons: An Anthology*. Edited by Albert C. Outler and Richard Heitzenrater. Nashville, TN: Abingdon Press.

Wesley, J. (1994). *The Works of John Wesley*. Edited by Thomas Jackson. CD Rom. Vol. XIV. Franklin, TN: Providence Hose.

Westfield, N.L. (2006). Mama Why..?' A Womanist Epistemology of Hope. In *Deeper Shades of Purple: Womanism in Religion and Society*, edited by Stacey Floyd-Thomas, 128–42. New York and London: New York University Press.

Westfield, N.L. (2013). Christian Education as Conversation. In *Under the Oak Tree: The Church as Community of Conversation in a Conflicted and Pluralistic World*, edited by Ronald J Allen, John S. McClure, and O. Wesley Allen, JR. Eugene, OR: Wipf and Stock Publishers.

Williams, D. (1993). *Sisters in the Wilderness: The Challenge of Womanist God-Talk*. Maryknoll, NY: Orbis Books.

Wimberly, A.E.S. (2005). *Soul Stories: African American Christian Education*. Revised. Nashville: Abingdon Press.

Wimberly, A.E.S., & Parker, E.L. (2002). *In Search of Wisdom: Faith Formation in the Black Church*. Nashville: Abingdon Press.

Wimberly, A.E.S., Barnes, S.L., & Johnson, K.D. (2013). *Youth Ministry in the Black Church: Centered in Hope*. Valley Forge, PA: Judson Press.